FOUNDATIONS OF MODERN ECONOMICS SERIES

Otto Eckstein, *Editor*

NEW VOLUMES

Prices and Markets, *Robert Dorfman*
Labor Economics, *John T. Dunlop*
Evolution of Modern Economics, *Richard T. Gill*
Economic Systems, *Gregory Grossman*
Managerial Economics, *Donald E. Farrar and John R. Meyer*

SECOND EDITIONS

American Industry: Structure, Conduct, Performance, *Richard Caves*
Money and Credit: Impact and Control, *James S. Duesenberry*
Public Finance, *Otto Eckstein*
Economic Development: Past and Present, *Richard T. Gill*
International Economics, *Peter B. Kenen*
National Income Analysis, *Charles L. Schultze*
Student Guide and Workbook for the Foundations of Modern Economic
  Series, *Hartman-Gustafson*

FIRST EDITION

The Price System, *Robert Dorfman*

FOUNDATIONS OF MODERN ECONOMICS SERIES

GREGORY GROSSMAN   *University of California, Berkeley*

Economic Systems

PRENTICE-HALL, INC.   *Englewood Cliffs, New Jersey*

PRENTICE-HALL FOUNDATIONS
OF MODERN ECONOMICS SERIES

Otto Eckstein, *Editor*

Current printing (last digit):
10   9   8   7   6

PRENTICE-HALL INTERNATIONAL INC., *London*

PRENTICE-HALL OF AUSTRALIA, PTY., LTD., *Sydney*

PRENTICE-HALL OF CANADA, LTD., *Toronto*

PRENTICE-HALL OF INDIA PVT. LTD., *New Delhi*

PRENTICE-HALL OF JAPAN, INC., *Tokyo*

C

Foundations

of Modern Economics Series

Economics has grown so rapidly in recent years, it has increased so much in scope and depth, and the new dominance of the empirical approach has so transformed its character, that no one book can do it justice today. To fill this need, the Foundations of Modern Economics Series was conceived. The Series, brief books written by leading specialists, reflects the structure, content, and key scientific and policy issues of each field. Used in combination, the Series provides the material for the basic one-year college course. The analytical core of economics is presented in *Prices and Markets* and *National Income Analysis,* which are basic to the various fields of application. *Prices and Markets,* a new book prepared especially for this edition of the Series, takes the beginning student through the elements of that subject step-by-step. *The Price System* is a more sophisticated alternative carried over from the first edition. Two books in the Series, *The Evolution of Modern Economics* and *Economic Development: Past and Present,* can be read without prerequisite and can serve as an introduction to the subject.

The Foundations approach enables an instructor to devise his own course curriculum rather than to follow the format of the traditional textbook. Once analytical principles have been mastered, many sequences of topics can be arranged and specific areas can be explored at length. An instructor not interested in a complete survey course can omit some books and concentrate on a detailed study of a few fields. One-semester courses stressing either macro-

or micro-economics can be readily devised. The instructors guide to the Series indicates the variety of ways the books in the Series can be used.

This Series is an experiment in teaching. The positive response to the first edition has encouraged us to continue, and to develop and improve, the approach. The thoughtful reactions of many teachers who have used the books in the past have been of immense help in preparing the second edition —in improving the integration of the Series, in smoothing some rough spots in exposition, and in suggesting additional topics for coverage.

The books do not offer settled conclusions. They introduce the central problems of each field and indicate how economic analysis enables the reader to think more intelligently about them, to make him a more thoughtful citizen, and to encourage him to pursue the subject further.

Otto Eckstein, Editor

Contents

Criteria and Values

CHAPTER ONE

INTRODUCTION

If you live in the United States, the food you buy is probably grown on a family farm, handled by private middlemen, processed by private companies, and sold to you by an independent grocer or a chain store. You have never met the farmers, the middlemen, and the processors, and you do not care to meet them. Nor do they care to meet you. But you do care that they and the grocers keep producing and selling the goods you want, and they and their employees and stockholders care that you keep buying what they have to sell. They do what they are doing for profits and wages, which they get by supplying you with what you are prepared to buy at prices you are prepared to pay.

The groceries that your Russian counterpart buys have been grown on a state farm or a collective farm; they were processed and moved by state enterprises and were probably sold in a state store.[1] The individual workers received wages for their work, or in the case of the collective farmers, a share of the net income; but they did what they did primarily because they were directed in great detail by the government and its planners.

In Yugoslavia, another communist country but with a radically different economic system from the Soviet, the food is grown by peasants, free to grow what they want. But it is processed, trans-

---

[1] As we shall see in Chapter 6, footnote 7, a considerable proportion of foodstuffs is purchased by Russian consumers directly from peasants.

ported, and sold by socialist enterprises in which, however, the workers and their representatives themselves decide what and how to produce without any direct orders from the government. They do so for the sake of profits, which in large measure go into their own pockets, and which they get (as do American firms) by meeting consumer demand in the market. And, finally, most of the population of the world still gets most of its food from the family's own field, or rice paddy, or livestock herd, without the intermediation of any outsiders.

These four instances illustrate the strikingly different ways in which people in different societies obtain their daily bread. Such differences, of course, are not limited to food; they extend to all the goods and services produced and consumed, to the distribution of income and wealth among the members of each society, to the growth and development of the economy, to the provision of society's collective needs, to the support of the needy and the individual's protection against insecurity, and so forth. The *way* these things are done has a lot to do with *how well* they are done and *what* gets done at all. Moreover, the way these things are done has a lot to do with how people order their social and political affairs in general, and with what they believe is right, just, and fair.

To put it differently, every economy has to accomplish certain basic tasks: determine what, where, how, and how much is to be produced; allocate the aggregate amount of goods and services produced (the "gross national product") between private consumption, collective consumption, replacement of capital stock used up in the course of production, and further growth of the economy; distribute its material benefits (the "national income") among the members of society; and maintain economic relations with the outside world. It may do these things spontaneously, with no central direction or planning, or with some measure of central control, but do them it must to be a functioning economy.

The simplest arrangement is for every household to take care directly of its own economic needs and be entirely independent of the rest of the community or society: to produce its own food, clothing, shelter, and other things; to distribute these within the family according to some customary notions; to take care of its own young, old, and invalids; and to fall back on its own resources in the face of insecurity. Instances of such a *subsistence economy* in its extreme form, with no exchange between households at all, would be hard to find nowadays; though less extreme forms, in which exchange does occur but on a very small scale, still exist in many parts of the underdeveloped world.

Whatever romantic qualities may attach to it, the subsistence economy has one fatal flaw—it is doomed to very low labor productivity and therefore to a very low level of consumption. Higher levels of living require higher labor productivity, which can be attained only with division of labor, specialization, exchange, and hence considerable interdependence among individuals or families. A modern, industrial, productive economy implies an extremely high degree of interdependence, a fact that the reader can easily confirm to his own satisfaction by stopping to reflect for a moment on the proportion of his material needs he himself supplies directly.

2

An economy in which individuals and families are substantially interdependent is usually called a *social economy*. It is only with the social economy, and only with the more advanced kinds, that this book concerns itself. In order to accomplish its tasks, a social economy resorts to what the social scientist calls *institutions*—an institution in its broadest sense being a set of "norms, rules of conduct, or established ways of thinking." [2] Property, the business corporation, the family household, the government, money, the income tax, sharecropping, the tipping of waiters, planning, profit-making, the labor union—these are all examples of economic institutions.

The set of institutions that characterizes a given economy comprises its *economic system*. To facilitate analysis, we may also deal with imaginary economic systems in which the institutions are kept deliberately "pure" and relatively simple. Imaginary systems of this kind, usually called *models,* can be very helpful in understanding real or potential institutions and systems.

Two more quick definitions: By *economic unit,* we mean a group of individuals such as a household, a firm, a labor union, or a government bureau brought together for a common economic purpose. By *economic agent,* we mean someone who performs a particular kind of economic function; e.g., a consumer, a worker, an entrepreneur, an investor, or a planner.

In studying economic systems, there is always the danger that we will fall victim to our own preconceptions, prejudices, and biases, or fall into nasty semantic traps. We shall gain little unless we try hard to keep our minds open. Being objective does not mean abandoning all preferences and values; this would be as unnecessary as it is unlikely. It does, however, mean making a strong effort to understand the logic, historical origins, and purposes of all kinds of institutions and ideas, whether we or our fellow citizens like them or not; avoiding easy labels; and, most of all, taking nothing for granted.

PERFORMANCE CRITERIA

Comparing economic systems, we inevitably ask which is best. But what does "best" mean in this context? It is difficult enough to tell which of several automobiles is best. Some of the criteria we apply to cars—purchase price, credit terms, operating cost, resale value—can be brought to the same denominator, dollars and cents, discounted to the same point in time, and combined into a single figure for each car, which can then be compared with corresponding figures for other cars. But other criteria—appearance, comfort, ease of handling, safety, snob appeal—cannot be reduced to a common denominator; and insofar as they enter into our decision, they do so through our subjective preferences. The preferences of different persons need not be alike, which is why there are so many different cars on the road.

Even more than evaluating cars, evaluating economic systems involves subjective preferences as well as rational appraisal. But unlike the criteria that apply to cars, the criteria that apply to economic systems include many

[2] Walter S. Buckingham, Jr., *Theoretical Economic Systems: A Comparative Analysis* (New York: Ronald Press, 1958), p. 90.

of the basic philosophic issues—welfare, progress, freedom, security, efficiency —on which reasonable men have disagreed for centuries and no doubt will continue to disagree for many more. Only the dogmatic will insist on applying a single yardstick to measure the performance of all economic systems. In the final analysis, it is up to each of us to decide which combination of features in an economic system we like best. Yet, in contrast to cars, each of us cannot have for himself the economic system he wants if it is different from the one that obtains in his society (unless, of course, the system of his choice exists in another country and he is willing to emigrate). To change an economic system, or to improve the existing one, or to preserve it, we have to resort to political action. Indeed, this is what a great deal of political action in a democracy is about.

A cautionary note. It is legitimate to compare ideal or pure systems, or actual economies, among themselves, or an actual system with *its own* ideal. It is not legitimate to compare an actual economy with an ideal model of a different kind (say, American reality with an abstract model of social-ism, or Soviet reality with an ideal capitalism), though exactly this trick is often resorted to by none-too-scrupulous or simply careless politicians and propagandists.

Plenty

Clearly, one of the first things we should like to know about economies with different systems is how much they produce or provide in goods and serv-ices, over-all and per person. Here we have a variety of measures to choose from: e.g., gross national income and consumption. We may wish to break these measures down even further—for instance, into industrial and agricul-tural output, or into private goods and collective goods, or into goods that sig-nificantly enhance defensive capacity and those that do not. We may also be interested in labor productivity: national product per gainfully employed per-son, or industrial production per man-hour. And let us not forget leisure (time free from work), an important product in every economy.

The particular criteria we employ will depend on the questions we wish to answer, unless the inadequacies of statistical data force us to resort to less appropriate measures, which is often the case. It should be noted, though, that the purely technical statistical problems of carrying out international com-parisons of this sort are very complex, and the numerical results, in which the man in the street often has considerable and understandable interest, can at times be properly interpreted only by those skilled in economic statistics.

Furthermore, the implications with regard to economic *systems* are not always obvious. Just because one country's production per capita is only, say, one-half of another country's does not mean that its system is correspondingly worse. A given economy's production per person depends not only on its in-stitutions but also on a large number of historical, cultural, geographic, nat-ural, and demographic circumstances as well. Because the American national product per capita is very much higher than the Soviet does no more *by itself* prove the superiority of "capitalism" over "socialism" than the fact that the national product per capita of "socialist" Czechoslovakia is much higher than that of "capitalist" Greece proves the reverse.

4

Growth

Today, more than in any previous era, growth is considered to be a major criterion of successful economic performance; indeed, in the eyes of many people in the world, it is the most important criterion.[3] In most of the hundred-odd underdeveloped countries, economic development, meaning primarily growth of production, often constitutes the major national purpose, at times to the point of obsession in the eyes of those of us who are more comfortably situated. In many of these countries, the success of their governments and institutions tends to be largely measured in terms of the growth that they produce or permit; while alternative systems vying for emulation and goodwill in these countries—capitalism and socialism, democracy and dictatorship —tend to be measured by the same yardstick.

Yet it is not simply the challenge from communism and the competition of the two politico-economic systems in the eyes of the "third world" nor solely the imperatives of national defense that have prompted the advanced Western countries to seek a steady and substantial rate of economic growth. There are sound domestic reasons for such an aim. Take the problem of poverty, for instance. Rich as these nations are over-all, none of them, not even the United States, is without significant—at times, shocking—pockets of poverty which are difficult to justify on social and moral grounds in otherwise relatively affluent societies. The elimination of such poverty calls for (a) structural changes, such as the movement of people out of, or the creation of jobs in, depressed sectors; (b) enlargement of employment opportunities in general; and (c) redistribution of income in favor of those individuals who, for various reasons, cannot benefit from the first two types of measures. All these measures, however, are politically much more feasible when the national income is growing rapidly than when it is growing slowly or not at all.

On the other hand, it would be wrong to assume that growth alone helps solve social problems. It may also be the chief cause of their appearance and aggravation, especially at early stages of industrialization when many of the old traditions, institutions, attitudes, and economic interests are destroyed or impaired. For this reason, economic development, especially rapid industrialization, may be resisted by various groups in society.[4]

Stability

Economic instability usually refers to two kinds of closely interrelated phenomena: periodic fluctuations in employment and output in the whole economy or some of its sectors (business fluctuations, business cycles), and persistent and significant upward or downward movement of prices in gen-

---

[3] A comprehensive discussion of economic growth in its historical and policy aspects may be found in *Economic Development: Past and Present* by Richard T. Gill, another volume in the *Foundations of Modern Economics Series*.

[4] What has already been said about the difficulties of measuring relative outputs applies even more to measuring comparative growth, where we introduce the time dimension and with it a whole set of additional conceptual and statistical difficulties.

eral (inflation or deflation). Inflation favors debtors and penalizes creditors, changes the relative well-being of economic classes, cuts into some forms of savings, and introduces greater uncertainty into economic decisions. Recessions and depressions have most of the inequitable and unfortunate effects of inflation and are often accompanied by deflation. In addition, they directly reduce the national product and real income of the whole society and throw people out of work, thus setting in motion accompanying human and social tragedies and costs. The propensity of the economy toward economic instability is clearly in large part a function of its institutions, and different economic systems may well differ on this score.

Security

In the more developed countries of today the individual household's economic security is no longer at the mercy of a fickle nature, as it had been until recently since the beginning of time, and as it still is in most of the underdeveloped world. But modern man has gained this security at the price of an immeasurably greater dependence on the rest of society. His insecurity now stems primarily from the unpredictability of social phenomena. Fortunately, these are not completely beyond society's control, nor need the individual be entirely without social protection against unexpected adversity.

A major type of individual economic insecurity derives from economic instability. But even in the absence of a depression or inflation, and often for no fault of his own, a person may lose his job, property, or earning power. Many such unfortunate events, especially if they have purely personal causes, cannot very well be prevented under any economic system. Insofar as they are the by-products of progress or of spontaneous shifts in consumer demand, it may not even be desirable to prevent them lest progress or the freedom of consumer choice be obstructed. And in addition there are the many and often tragic risks of sickness, invalidity, death of the breadwinner, and so forth.

By and large public opinion in modern, advanced countries (and even in many poorer countries) nowadays agrees that people should not bear the full brunt of adverse social forces and "acts of God" over which they have no control. It is this emphasis on the protection of the individual against various risks that is one of the main distinguishing features of the twentieth century as compared with former centuries. Those states which underwrite a wide range of such risks, and perhaps furnish a large number of other services to their citizens, are usually referred to as "welfare states," although the term tends to be used very loosely. In regard to individual security, economic systems vary, first, in the extent to which they are (or are not) welfare states, and second, in the extent to which they do or do not attempt to prevent the social causes of insecurity, such as business fluctuations.

Efficiency

Few of us are against efficiency, and even fewer are for its opposite, waste. The economist recognizes three kinds of efficiency. First, there is technical efficiency, the most effective use of a given resource (labor, material, machine, etc.) *in a particular job*. Waste is exemplified by labor idling on the job, excessive fuel burned under a boiler, materials spoiling because of neglect, or a motor running unnecessarily. It may seem at first glance that technical inefficiency has little to do with economic institutions—at least we take the desire to avoid it for granted. But in point of fact the avoidance of technical inefficiency depends a great deal on incentives to managers and workers, which in turn rests on socio-economic institutions. For instance, technical inefficiency is a very serious problem in Soviet-type economies, as we shall see in Chapter 6. More subtly, economic systems may be associated with different attitudes towards thriftiness and work discipline.

There are two kinds of economic efficiency, static and dynamic. *Static economic efficiency* subsumes technical efficiency and represents the best allocation of available resources among all the alternative uses in a given time span. In other words, economic efficiency obtains when no possible reallocation of resources can increase the output of one or more final goods without at the same time decreasing the output of one or more final goods. It is of course an ideal that is probably not even closely approached by any actual economy, but nonetheless the notion is a very useful one for analytical purposes.[5]

How efficiently a given economy (or an economic model) actually does (or might) operate depends on the nature of prices, the rules for decision-making that obtain among managers and planners, the degree of centralization of decisions, the degree of competition, the fiscal structure, and many other factors. Clearly, these in turn largely depend on the economy's institutions.

Dynamic efficiency, on the other hand, relates economic growth to the increase in resources that supposedly occasions this growth. Thus, two economies may both increase their stocks of capital by some percentage, their labor forces by some percentage, and so forth, and yet the rate of growth of the national product in the two cases may be quite different. As with differences in productivity, the difference in dynamic efficiency may also stem from differences in the ease with which the two economies adopt economically rational innovations, or in the extent to which their *static* efficiencies change as they grow, and so forth. These, in turn, may derive primarily from the systems' institutions.

Equity and Justice; Equality

Rare is the man who does not have some notion of what is or is not fair or just in the distribution of income, wealth, power, and opportunity among individuals and groups in society. Almost equally rare is the man who does not feel strongly about it. We are all prone to judge political and economic systems by the criterion of distributive justice and equity. At bottom, every "ism" assumes some standard of social justice (as it also assumes some image of human nature), and every reform or revolution, or opposition to them, is motivated primarily by distributive considerations.

But considerations of equity and justice are not the only ones applicable

[5] Chapter 6 of Robert Dorfman's *The Price System,* this series, addresses itself at greater length to what we here call static economic efficiency. Notice that efficiency in this sense is not the same as productivity, which depends on the level of technology and the quality of available resources as well as on the efficiency with which these two factors are utilized.

in this connection. Income, wealth, power, and opportunity are also incentives for productive activity. A more equal distribution of these benefits in society may in some measure be at the expense of efficiency, productivity, and growth. Most of us will probably agree that there is no formula that will finely balance the ethical requirements of distributive justice against the needs of productivity and growth. Each of us has to find the answer within himself, and our attitudes to different institutions and economic systems will be shaped accordingly.

Economic Freedoms

Much belabored and abused, the word "freedom" may mean different things and refer to many different conditions. We use the word here in the sense of absence of social obstacles to effective choice, and for the moment we concern ourselves only with "economic freedom"—or, better, "economic freedoms," since there are several.

Choice may be exercised by different kinds of economic unit and economic agent. Let us begin with *households:* If in their capacity as consumers they are free to buy any goods available for purchase (of course within the limits of their purchasing power or credit), the condition known as *freedom of consumer choice* exists. This freedom is absent if, to a significant extent, consumers are limited in their purchases by rationing (as in wartime in the United States or elsewhere) or if they are doled out goods in predetermined amounts (as happened in Russia during so-called period of War Communism, 1918-1921). If individuals are essentially free to accept any job within the limits of their abilities and to quit any job, they enjoy *freedom of choice of job.* In most societies this freedom is less fully realized than the freedom of consumer choice because of professional degree requirements, formal licensing of professions, restrictions imposed by unions, military service, and so on. These two freedoms, plus the freedom to make use of whatever other resources the household may dispose of, make up *freedom of household choice.*

Similarly, a business enterprise (which at times is not distinguishable from a household) may have the freedom to acquire any resources it wishes and can pay for, to use any technology (within the limits imposed by patent laws), to produce any products, to sell them at any price it can charge, and to invest in any way it pleases. If it can do all these things, it enjoys maximum *freedom of enterprise.* In reality, it usually cannot do all these things as it pleases. It may be restricted by labor laws and collective bargaining contracts, zoning regulations, sanitary and building codes, provisions of the corporate charter, price controls, and so forth *ad infinitum.* Freedom of enterprise is always relative. Still, in some countries or economic systems there is so much more of it than in others that we can meaningfully speak of "free enterprise economies (or systems)." Notice that free enterprise is not identical with private enterprise. *Private* enterprise need not be very free; it was not under the Nazis in Germany. On the other hand, a publicly owned enterprise may be just as free in its business activities as its private counterpart, as exemplified by two French automotive concerns: Renault, a nationalized company, and Peugeot, a private one.

Freedom of household choice and freedom of enterprise may be valued *per se.* Americans, especially, in line with our individualistic tradition, feel that individuals (or households) and businesses should be free to spend their own money as they see fit and to do as they wish with the resources at their command, so long as they do not thereby seriously impair society's interests and well-being.

However, many would also add that people and businesses cannot be regarded identically for this purpose, because in the final analysis businesses exist for people, and not *vice versa*. Furthermore, many would insist that among businesses one must sharply distinguish between small, personal enterprises and large (and typically bureaucratic and impersonal) corporations.[6] By virtue of its size, importance, impact on the economy, and impersonal nature, the large corporation is often regarded as a quasi-public body.[7]

But in addition to being valuable in their own right, freedom of household choice and freedom of enterprise have also *instrumental* importance. They are highly useful social devices that permit consumers to get the most for their incomes [8] and facilitate (though do not ensure) efficient use of resources and the exercise of initiative by business firms.

Economic Sovereignty

Who ultimately decides what will be produced by the economy? If it is consumers—say, by exercising effective demand in the market—and if production is closely attuned to consumer preferences, then the economist says that *consumers' sovereignty* prevails.[9] In fact, because the preferences of households as resource owners (especially, as suppliers of labor) also affect production, it is better to speak of *household sovereignty*. On the other hand, most things may be produced in response to the explicit preferences or wishes of the country's political leaders—as for instance in the Soviet Union—in which case we speak of the dominance of *leaders' preferences* or of *leaders' sovereignty*.[10]

Consumers' sovereignty should not be confused with freedom of con-

[6] Although the corporation is a "legal person" in that it can sue and be sued, it can hardly be identified for most purposes with an individual or a small, private business. To do so would be to commit what Thurman W. Arnold has called "the personification of the corporation"; see his *The Folklore of Capitalism* (Garden City, N.Y.: Blue Ribbon Books, 1937), Chapter VIII. This book, though by now somewhat dated in its factual material, is still a most stimulating discussion of the myths and fallacies that often block our understanding of economic matters. A more recent critique along similar lines is Dow Votaw's "The Mythology of Corporations," *California Management Review*, Vol. IV, No. 3 (Spring, 1962), pp. 58-74.

[7] We return to this point in Chapter 4.

[8] Institutionally, the opposite of free consumers' choice is the rationing of consumer goods, typically by means of ration cards or coupons, as in the U.S. during World War II. Although warranted in emergency situations, rationing is inconvenient for consumers, encourages black-marketeering and other violations of law, seriously impairs legitimate economic incentives, and is costly for society to administer and enforce. For these reasons even communist regimes prefer to maintain freedom of consumer choice in normal times.

[9] Notice that consumers' sovereignty has only limited bearing on consumer welfare. The Soviet consumer exercises little economic sovereignty but is materially better off than the Ethiopian consumer, who does.

[10] Also sometimes (and less correctly) referred to as *planners'* preferences and *planners'* sovereignty.

sumer choice. Sovereignty refers to the ultimate source of production decisions; consumer choice, to the method by which the produced consumer goods are distributed to households. For example, central planners may themselves determine what and how much is produced, thus denying sovereignty to consumers, but may rely on free choice at the retail level—on a "take it or leave it" basis—to distribute consumer goods to individual households, of course within the limits of each household's income. Such a combination of the absence of consumers' sovereignty with the presence of freedom of consumer choice obtains in the USSR.

Although it is sometimes said that consumers' sovereignty prevails in a country such as the United States, the statement can be accepted only with major qualifications. (1) Numerous factors—taxes, monopoly power, limitations on resource mobility—interpose themselves between consumer demand and production, so that the latter is far from perfectly attuned to the former. (2) In certain cases governments interfere directly with consumption; for example, forbidding the use of narcotics or requiring a minimum amount of education for each citizen. (3) Only some two-thirds of the final demand in the American economy originates with consumers. About one-fifth of the gross national product is taken by all levels of government; this final demand is not determined by consumers as consumers. The remainder of the gross national product, about 15 per cent, goes for business investment, which in turn looks forward to future demand by consumers, government, and business.

Whether consumers' sovereignty is a desirable feature of an economic system or not has been debated a good deal among economists, especially among proponents of different kinds of socialism during the nineteen thirties and forties. Democratic socialists, in common with other democratically-inclined social scientists and statesmen, consider it desirable, despite the several qualifications just listed. Authoritarian socialists, especially communists, put little stock in it. Generally speaking, the arguments have been as follows. *Pro consumers' sovereignty:* (1) Production is for people, for consumers, and therefore their desires and preferences should be decisive in the final analysis. (2) Consumers know best what's best for them, although they may need a good deal of education on this score as well as protection against quackery and fraud. (3) Disregard of consumers' sovereignty may open the door to other kinds of authoritarianism, especially political dictatorship. *Against consumers' sovereignty* the arguments have been: (1) Consumers often do not know what is best for them because they lack the necessary scientific and technical information, or because they do not care. (2) Tastes of different consumers are not independent but are swayed by fads and fashions. (3) Nor is consumer demand spontaneous, for it is heavily influenced by advertising and other pressure from producers. (4) The average consumer does not appreciate the distant future sufficiently and does not save enough for later generations.[11] (5) Consumer demand depends heavily on the distribution of income and wealth—i.e., the consumers' "dollar ballots" are of unequal urgency to them and it is improper to speak of consumer sovereignty without reference to income distribution. The upholders of consumers' sovereignty admit many of these strictures but prefer to deal with the problems in ways other

[11] This point is of course more important in the poorer countries, which badly need to build up their productive capital.

than rejecting consumer sovereignty outright—for example, by consumer education, letting society (government) add to the level of saving in the economy, and redistributing incomes through taxation and other democratic means in order to make the "dollar ballots" more comparable.

The criteria that we have discussed so far have been, if not narrowly economic, primarily so. But man does not live by bread alone; he does not judge alternative socio-economic systems only by their material aspects. He tests them in the crucible of his ethical, religious, and political beliefs. Material success itself may be looked upon with suspicion as distorting human values and standing in the way of what is considered to be the ideal of a good society on ethical grounds.

Thus, the "utopian socialists" of the first half of the nineteenth century and the Christian socialists of the twentieth century rejected what they believed to be the excessive materialism, money-grubbing, and social injustices of capitalism.[12] Proponents of capitalism, on the other hand, have upheld it not only for its material results but also for its likely beneficial effects on individual initiative, individual self-reliance, and political freedom. At times they have even admitted that on economic grounds alone capitalism may leave something to be desired but have held the loss to be a small material price to pay for the strengthening of political freedom.[13]

The case for capitalism as a promoter of political freedom is essentially twofold. First, the rise and spread of political liberty in the modern world has largely paralleled the rise and development of capitalism. Secondly, liberty fares best in those societies in which power is least concentrated; the market and private property are effective institutions for keeping power unconcentrated (chiefly, by reducing the power of the state). Moreover, the market mechanism is impersonal; it amounts to a "rule of law (economic rules) and not of men" in the economic sphere. On the other hand, obviously capitalism does not *guarantee* liberty; even today in many countries it goes hand in hand with dictatorship.

VALUES

The performance criteria just listed are not merely yardsticks for comparing different economic systems or means for attaining other things.

[12] One of the most eloquent—and by now classic—indictments of capitalistic materialism from a Christian-ethical standpoint is *The Acquisitive Society* (New York: Harcourt, Brace, 1920) by the late eminent British economic historian and Fabian socialist R. H. Tawney. See also Chapter 3.

[13] A good statement of this position may be found in Henry C. Wallich's *The Cost of Freedom: Conservatives and Modern Capitalism* (New York: Harper, 1960). Less moderate statements in defense of capitalism as a promoter of political freedom will be found in two classic works, both by University of Chicago economists: Friedrich A. Hayek, *The Road to Serfdom* (Chicago: University of Chicago Press, 1944); and Milton Friedman, *Capitalism and Freedom* (Chicago: University of Chicago Press paperback, 1962).

Most of them may be and often are desired for their own sakes as *goals* or *ends* of social life, and as such they become social *values*. Unlike the choice among purely instrumental means, the choice between alternative ends or values cannot be made on the basis of a rational calculus. Values cannot be reduced to a common denominator, nor can one value be logically demonstrated to be superior to another. Insofar as accepted, they are accepted as matters of faith, belief, philosophy, or whim.

In fact, most people tend to accept the same individual values. Most people in all societies are for plenty, for freedom, and for individual security. Where they differ is in the relative importance attached to them and in the willingness to sacrifice a measure of one (for themselves or for others) for a measure of the other. On this score they may not only differ, but often differ violently.

Values often tend to be interdependent in the sense that some social ends conflict with one another. We can realize one of them more fully only if we give up a measure of another. At other times they complement one another. Striving for one of them, we also facilitate the realization of another. Let us illustrate with reference to growth as a goal of social policy. Thus, growth and social justice may well conflict under certain conditions. In order to step up the rate of economic growth, we may find it necessary to sacrifice a measure of equality in the distribution of income, wealth, and power. First, under socialism as well as under capitalism, growth is spurred if those who contribute more to it are also rewarded with more. Under socialism, individuals may be limited in the amount of wealth they are permitted to accumulate and in the ways they may employ it, but they are still likely to acquire power in other forms. Moreover, the more rapid the growth, the larger must be the proportion of national income saved, which is often more easily accomplished with a more unequal distribution of income. Should growth call for a strong national political leadership, so much the greater the concentration of power in the society. The causation works the other way as well: The more rapid the growth, the greater the structural changes, the more are traditions broken, the greater the disequilibria—hence the greater also the opportunities for some individuals to earn large incomes, to accumulate wealth, and to amass power.

CHAPTER TWO

COORDINATING MECHANISMS

Every economic unit in a social economy is dependent on innumerable other units to furnish it with consumer goods, labor services, materials, fuel, and markets for its products. Without some mechanism to provide the minimal amount of coordination of the activities of the separate but interdependent economic units, a modern economy would not be able to meet even the most basic needs of its citizens. Moreover, this mechanism should not only bring the various factors of production into productive use, but should ensure that their employment be tolerably full and efficient. Finally, it should distribute incomes to consumers—that is, to all of us—in a tolerably equitable way.

There are three such coordinating mechanisms, generally speaking: tradition, the market mechanism, and command.

Tradition

By tradition we mean generally accepted, customary, and persistent specific patterns of relationship among economic units or agents. In relatively primitive economies a very large part of economic life is often so governed: exchange between individuals or tribes; the individual's occupation within the existing division of labor; the tribute paid to authority; and so forth. Thus, in a medieval manor, tradition determined the relations between the payments of the serfs to the lord in labor, produce, or money; his

13

reciprocal obligations to the serfs; and the support he furnished to other members of the manor community (priests, artisans, servants). As this example shows, the origin of the traditional relationship may be traceable to certain power relations or initial bargains, but with time these become crystallized into customary relationships that are generally accepted most of the time. In a modern economy, the role of tradition is relatively much smaller but by no means negligible. Private charity and philanthropy, tipping, many aspects of employer-employee relations, the exchange of gifts and favors, the ethics and limits of competitive behavior, professional standards—these and many other norms of behavior are governed in large measure by tradition.

As a mechanism for regulating the division of labor and the distribution of benefits and burdens in society, tradition has many advantages, perhaps the most important of which is the predictability of the relations and behavior patterns in question. It saves the need for renegotiating individual transactions, while at the same time avoiding the unpleasant element of compulsion that may often attach to command. Its chief drawback is obviously the slowness with which it adjusts to changing conditions—technological innovations, new products, new tastes and mores, changing notions of justice and equity— if it adjusts to them at all. It is thus often an obstacle to progress, especially in the early stages of industrialization when the traditional ties and norms of behavior are still strong.[1] Yet at times the preservation of some measure of tradition may actually facilitate orderly transition to a modern economy and society by taking the edge off social instability and individual insecurity occasioned by rapid modernization.[2]

Market Mechanism

However, in all more or less advanced economies (other than those of the Soviet type), it is chiefly the market mechanism that allocates resources among various lines of activity; adjusts production, consumption, and resources to one another; distributes incomes; and brings about economic growth. The market mechanism (sometimes also called "the price mechanism" or "the price system"[3] or simply "the market") has been at the center of economists' attention for centuries, yet there is no standard definition of it. We may say that the *market mechanism* operates in a social economy when the following three conditions are met: (1) The individual economic units by and large decide themselves what, how, where, and when they produce and consume. (2) They do so largely with reference to the terms on which alternatives are available to them—i.e., with reference to *prices* in the broadest sense of the word. (3) Prices respond, more or less, to the forces of demand and supply for the individual goods or factors. The end result tends to be the equilibration of demand and supply and the coordination of the economic activities of innumerable individual units and agents.

[1] Cf. the discussion by Richard T. Gill, *Economic Development: Past and Present,* 2nd ed., this series, pp. 30-31.

[2] Such have been the case with the highly paternalistic employer-employee relations that have persisted in Japan despite very rapid industrialization over the better part of a century. See James C. Abegglen, *The Japanese Factory* (Glencoe, Ill.: The Free Press, 1958).

[3] This is the phrase preferred by Robert Dorfman in his book in this series *The Price System,* to whom we leave the analytical treatment of the operation of the market mechanism.

Too much should not be read into this definition. For instance, it says nothing about whether firms are privately or publicly owned; nor about the degree or character of competition among the firms or households; nor about the rules which the individual economic agents follow in making their decisions; nor about the presence and extent of government intervention in the economy (so long as this intervention does not eliminate the market mechanism); nor about the price-forming process or degree of price responsiveness and flexibility; nor, finally, about the efficiency with which the economy's resources are used or allocated, or whether they are fully employed. But the definition does indicate that the economic units are largely independent or autonomous with regard to the decisions in question, and that they deal with one another primarily through voluntary exchange of goods and services. More or less automatically and impersonally, in highly complex economies as well as in relatively simple ones, day after day, the market mechanism—Adam Smith's "invisible hand"—directs and coordinates the decisions and activities of millions of independent, dispersed economic units and agents. With all its problems and imperfections, it is surely one of the most remarkable of social institutions. We shall return to inquire into some of the characteristics and problems of the market mechanism in Chapters 4 and 5.

Command

Yet the same directing, resource allocating, coordinating, and income distributing functions can be accomplished in a social economy by means that are in a sense the very opposite of the automatic and impersonal market mechanism; namely, by means of the *command principle* (or "command" for short). In this instance, the individual economic units (though probably only the firms and not the households) are ordered what, when, where, how, and how much to produce and consume. If done rationally at all, these commands (directives, orders, targets, "plans") derive from some sort of conscious attempt ("planning") to coordinate the activities of the individual units and to direct the economy as a whole toward certain definite goals.

The command principle implies several important things: relatively little independence or autonomy on the part of the individual economic unit; the presence of superior authority that issues the commands and is capable of eliciting a minimal degree of compliance; very probably a hierarchical organizational structure; and a minimal amount of *coordinative planning* on which the commands are based.

KINDS
OF ECONOMIC SYSTEMS

According to Mechanism

One way to distinguish among economic systems is according to the prevailing coordinating mechanism. While it is possible to devise abstract models of economic systems that contain only one of the three social mechanisms, actual contemporary economies (except the most primitive) contain all three in varying proportions. However, one of the social mechanisms usually predominates; accordingly, we speak of a *traditional economy, a market economy,* or *a command economy.*

Since in this book we limit our attention to modern economic systems, we shall not be concerned with the traditional economy hereafter. Rather, we shall focus our attention on the market economy (Chapters 4, 5 and 7) and the command economy (Chapter 6), always remembering, though, that tradition as a social mechanism may exist to an appreciable extent in either.

According to Ownership

Another major way in which economic systems differ is according to the prevailing ownership of productive assets. *"Capitalism"* is, of course, a system in which productive assets are privately owned—though private property is not a simple and clear-cut concept, as we shall presently see. *"Socialism"* has many definitions; [4] for the moment we shall think of it as an economic system in which most productive assets are publicly owned, usually by the state or some division thereof. The term "mixed economy" is often applied to an economy in which there are substantial amounts of both private and public ownership side by side.

It used to be thought that every capitalist economy would be governed by the market mechanism, and every socialist economy would forswear the market mechanism in favor of command. True, virtually all capitalist economies that have existed in history have been market economies; but the Nazi economy in Germany (say, between 1936 and 1945) may be called a capitalist command economy. And while most socialist economies—those under communist control—have been command economies most of the time, there is the important historical case of the USSR in the twenties and even the more important contemporary instance of Yugoslavia since the early fifties, both of which have been socialist market economies. [5]

But before taking up the various economic systems in some detail, we must take a look at certain institutions, which we do for the rest of this chapter.

POWER, PROPERTY, BUREAUCRACY

Power

Power is the capacity to influence the actions of others in a predictable way. Its distribution—or maldistribution—is clearly one of the chief criteria by which economic systems are judged. Its sources are many, since anything that can significantly influence the behavior of people can be translated into power by someone else.

A major source of power in any society is control over property, whether

---

[4] See Chapter 3.

[5] On the Yugoslav economic system see Chapter 7. Its importance is greatly enhanced by the possibility that a number of other communist countries may well abandon or modify the command system they now follow and move in the direction of the Yugoslav model.

private or public. To an orthodox Marxist, this is *the* source of power in the final analysis. To be sure, in a capitalist society private property is an important source of power. Yet its very prevalence may cause power to be diffused. Moreover, not all property interests coincide. The conflicts among them, as well as among them and labor and other large organized interests, are not only among the major conflicts in a democratic capitalist society but ensure the very dispersal of power (pluralism) that in the long run is the best safeguard of political democracy.

Another major kind of power is that which inheres in government. It reaches its highest concentration when both government and most productive property are under the control of the same individual or group, as in the communist countries.

In modern societies power also rests with important positions in administrative bureaucracies; with those in control of information flow (national intelligence services, the press and other communication media, sometimes also with the statistical services); with those in possession of scientific and technical expertise; with control over armed forces or other organs of coercion; with the ability to bring to bear the weight of large numbers of individuals (as in the case of labor unions, mass political parties, or other large organized groups); with moral authority (e.g., clergymen or some philosophers and statesmen) or the ability to manipulate ideological symbols (as in the case of politicians and demagogues); and with sheer personal qualities. The fact that one kind of power may dominate another—money may bribe legislators or bureaucrats, and business or labor can be dominated by a strong government—does not basically vitiate the fact that there is more than one *source* of power.

Property

Strictly speaking, *property* refers to a bundle of rights over tangible or intangible assets which permits the owner (within certain important limits to be presently noted) the right of use and disposal over them. In the case of *private* property, this right rests with private individuals; but the notion can be extended to include ownership by other non-governmental bodies, such as cooperatives and mutual societies. In this section we are concerned only with ownership of productive assets (means of production). The ownership of strictly consumers' goods by households is a form of private property that is often designated as "personal property." Only in some extreme and quite rare types of communist communities—though not in the present-day communist countries—is the individual not allowed to own personal property. As we have mentioned, whether the means of production in an economy are predominantly owned privately or by public (governmental) bodies is one of the most important distinguishing features of economic systems, even if—contrary to what is still maintained by the more extreme partisans on both sides—the factor of ownership does not determine everything of importance about an economic system.

17

The bounds of private property are not always sharp. From the *social* standpoint, the difference between certain specific privately and publicly owned production facilities is not very great. Think of a private urban bus line, subject to close control by municipal or state regulating authorities, and a bus line owned by a specially created public transit district. Here the rights attaching to private property (the bus company, though not necessarily the individually owned shares of stock in the company) are so circumscribed by government as to make the distinction between public and private enterprise quite tenuous. The situation is typical of many public utilities regulated by state, federal, or other public authorities.

This example leads to a more general observation. The use of privately owned assets is always and in many ways subject to innumerable restrictions and limitations imposed by various public authorities. In the United States these include, among many others, property and income taxes, which cut into the benefits obtainable from private ownership; zoning regulations; building, housing, safety, and sanitary codes; nuisance abatement regulations; and labor laws and regulations, which may substantially limit the use of property through restrictions on the employment contract. In certain cases the owner of the property is legally obligated to furnish its services regardless of his wishes; e.g., in the case of common carriers and public utilities (where the state, on the other hand, allows a certain return on capital in the setting of rates) and under the various state and federal anti-discrimination statutes. Lastly, the state always has the power of eminent domain—i.e., of forcing the owner to sell his property to the state or a division thereof for legitimate public purposes against (supposedly) fair compensation.

The brief list in the preceding paragraph is sufficient to show that in fact there is no such thing as an absolute right of private property. Nor is there likely to be in any actual society, however strongly it may be ideologically committed to private property and private enterprise, because of the great variety of social goals and values which in practice must be mutually reconciled and compromised.

Turning now to the social functions that the institution of private property performs, we might mention, first, that it plays a major role in determining the distribution of wealth, income, and power in society. In doing so it also helps determine the degree of decentralization of economic decisions. Second, private ownership is a most important device for preserving and maintaining society's capital (i.e., physical production facilities and stocks of goods, as well as claims on other countries), for the obvious reason that every owner looks after his own. Third, the desire to accumulate private property is a very powerful stimulus—historically, the most important one—for the continued increase in society's real capital, and for all economic activity. And last, private property performs the important *social* function of providing the individual and his dependents with economic security—provided of course he owns some to begin with and does not lose it at the crucial time (such as during a stock market crash)—and in this way contributes to the individual's over-all sense of independence.

In all these respects the institution of private property is only a means to certain ends, not an end in itself. As a means it is usually not without rivals. For instance, much new capital formation in capitalist countries—let alone the communist countries—is undertaken by governments nowadays. Even in such a staunchly capitalist country as the United States, about a fifth of all capital formation is in the public sector. Examples are roads, streets, schools, and public housing. Moreover, most of this capital stock is seemingly no worse maintained for being publicly owned.[6]

Drive; Incentives

Clearly, every economy must contain some source of drive. That the individual peasant, farmer, trader, artisan, or worker will pursue his trade or stick to his job in order to earn his own and his dependents' living is obvious enough. But why will people act as entrepreneurs, promoting and expanding businesses, or as managers of large enterprises, or as planners or industrializing statesmen? In regard to private enterprise we usually credit the *profit motive*—backed up by the institution of private property—with being the most important, if not the sole, source of drive. But what complex of psychological, cultural, and social elements lies behind the profit motive? Is it rooted in the "Protestant Ethic," as the great German sociologist Max Weber brilliantly—but not entirely convincingly—argued?[7] Is it a natural desire of the typical "economic man," as the classical economists assumed? And besides, how far will the profit motive push people along the lines of economic activity? We do not fully know the answers to these questions.

We do know that the profit motive in the usual sense is not the only motive force in economic life. The manager of a large corporation, who is the dominant type of manager and entrepreneur in the U.S. today, gets relatively little direct benefit from the profits that his organization earns. He takes his reward in salary and bonuses, partly in the dividends on the relatively small amount of the company's stock he may own, and no doubt also significantly in esteem. Others in executive positions—such as managers of public enterprises in the West and of firms in the Soviet Union, civil servants, national planners—work, at times extremely conscientiously and ably, for their salaries, occasional bonuses, professional pride, ideological convictions, national ideals, and various other non-profit motives.

Bureaucracy

Most important in any modern economy is the institution we usually call "formal organization." Business firms, except the very smallest, are instances of formal organizations, as are government departments, schools, labor unions, some churches, and so forth. An understanding of the way organizations function and the problems they face is therefore very important for the appreciation of economic systems. For instance, the Soviet-type command economy is one huge formal organization that takes in just about the whole economy with the exception of the household sector.

[6] Further observations on the social function of private property will be found in Chapter 4.

[7] *The Protestant Ethic and the Spirit of Capitalism,* translated by Talcott Parsons (New York: Scribners, 1930). A convenient summary of the controversy in this matter and suggestions for further reading will be found in Robert W. Green (ed.), *Protestantism and Capitalism: The Weber Thesis and its Critics* (Boston: Heath, 1959).

The mechanism that gets things done in a formal organization is generally referred to as a *bureaucracy*. The characteristics and problems of bureaucracies have been the objects of intensive study by social scientists in recent years, following the pioneering theoretical work on the subject in the early part of this century by Max Weber. An abstract model of a bureaucracy [8] contains the following feature. It has different levels of authority; its work is governed by definite and impersonal rules; each official in a bureaucracy has his own job and his own rules to apply; the officials are selected and appointed according to their qualifications for the jobs, and promoted according to their skill at applying the rules.

Such a bureaucracy is, theoretically speaking, a very efficient means for performing tasks in society, in that its work is expert, predictable (given the rules), and presumably speedy. But even the idealized model contains some drawbacks. The officials may see the problems that they tackle in only partial perspective and the rules may not keep pace with changing conditions. Actual bureaucracies may of course have many other defects that need not be spelled out here. Yet for many social tasks there is no practicable alternative to bureaucratic handling; consider military organizations, government departments, or large business firms.

Interestingly, the economy is one social sphere in which there does exist a successful alternative to the bureaucratic organization of complex tasks; namely, the market mechanism. In the economic sphere, in contrast to other social spheres, it is possible (1) to quantify the alternatives facing a decision-making unit—i.e., to express them in terms of prices; and (2) to define the goals of the unit in more or less definite and quantitative terms—e.g., profit-making. When these two conditions are met, the market mechanism can take over. Thus, a large American corporation may so decentralize its operations that its various divisions become virtually autonomous and are related to one another through a kind of internal market mechanism. The General Motors Corporation is a classic example of such corporate decentralization.[9] Or a Soviet-type command economy may dismantle its hierarchical structure, largely eliminate the command principle, and "marketize" itself, which is just what happened in Yugoslavia in the early nineteen-fifties.[10]

CENTRALIZATION-
DECENTRALIZATION

Economic systems differ very markedly in the degree of centralization that attends decisions and functions within them. As we have seen, a mar-

[8] On the Weberian model of a bureaucracy see, for example, Joseph A. Litterer (ed.), *Organizations: Structure and Behavior* (New York: Wiley, 1963). See also Robert K. Merton *et al.*, *Reader in Bureaucracy* (Glencoe, Ill.: The Free Press, 1952).

[9] The best known study of decentralization in the General Motors Corporation is Peter F. Drucker's *The Concept of the Corporation* (New York: John Day, 1946; Mentor Books paperback, 1964).

[10] On the other hand, there may also be good reasons for preserving a bureaucratic structure even where the organization could conceivably "marketize" itself internally. These reasons are typically related to the advantages of centralization, which are about to be taken up in the section. The advantages of a command economy over a market economy will be discussed in Chapter 6.

ket economy is a decentralized system in comparison with a command economy, but the degree of centralization (or decentralization) in each of these may also vary greatly. In a command economy, as in any formal organization, centralization (decentralization) means essentially the moving of decisions and functions to some higher (lower) level(s) in the formal hierarchy. In a market economy, where there is no over-all formal hierarchy, centralization of economic decisions and functions means either (1) their transfer from the independent economic units to some governmental body, or (2) their transfer from a lower governmental level to a higher one (e.g., from the local authority to the state government, or from the state to the federal government), or (3) to a higher level within the given governmental hierarchy.

Notice that there is always a cost attached to obtaining and processing information and maintaining communication lines, and, other things equal, the more centralized the organization (or economy) the greater this cost. In fact, a large part of the resource commitment in any type of modern economy is devoted to this end.[11] The choice between more and less centralized economic institutions therefore hinges in some measure on the corresponding information cost. It follows that a major technological advance in this area, such as the invention and development of electronic computers for the storage and high-speed processing and retrieval of information, coupled with up-to-date means of high-speed communication, tends to make a greater degree of centralization more attractive. Some large U.S. corporations have been lately centralizing operations thanks to computers, and there is great interest along these lines in the Soviet Union, where the handling of information is voluminous and costly, and where the preference for centralization is strong on doctrinal and political grounds.

Advantages of Decentralization

In the Western democratic countries, however, and especially in the United States, there is a strong general preference for decentralizing economic decisions and functions in society, in common with the preference for political decentralization. The reasons are not only, perhaps not mainly, economic. Thus, decentralization of economic functions within the context of a market economy tends to contribute to the dispersion of power, which in turn, as we have seen, tends to strengthen the bases of political and personal freedom. For those who make the decisions, it tends to make their work more satisfying, heightens their sense of responsibility and independence, promotes initiative and resourcefulness, and presumably contributes to the mature discharge of democratic responsibilities. These are realized best in a market economy and with a high degree of freedom of choice and opportunity.

But there are also more strictly economic considerations in favor of decentralization. Generally speaking, as we have mentioned, decentralization

[11] The student may wish to list for himself by way of exercise the occupations and institutions in the American economy that are primarily concerned with collecting, processing, and transmitting the information on which economic decisions are based. Then consult Fritz Machlup, *The Production and Distribution of Knowledge in the United States* (Princeton: Princeton University Press, 1962).

means shorter channels of communication; hence, lower cost, greater speed, and less risk of distortion in handling information—most important considerations where adaptation to changing conditions (fluctuations in demand, technical innovations) and speed of response play an important role, especially in competitive situations. This is what we mean when we say that those "on the spot" can decide many things much better and much faster than can their superiors in a formal organization or some government official in a bureau. It is precisely with regard to this kind of adaptation, flexibility, and speed of response that the Soviet economy, with its very long lines of communication, tends to perform quite poorly. Moreover, to the extent that excessive centralization dampens incentives, initiative, and responsibility, it tends to justify itself and perhaps even to prompt further centralization. Here, again, the Soviet example is apposite.

Advantages of Centralization

It would be wrong, however, to consider that all the advantages lie on the side of decentralization, as our pro-democratic biases might lead us to think, or that the arguments for centralization rest primarily on anti-democratic or power-grabbing instincts. Without ruling out these factors, we ought to recognize some very weighty reasons for centralization, whether within formal organizations (including the command economy) or in market economies.

One important reason is the need to safeguard or promote public interest and priorities. In all societies and organizations, the interests and values of particular individuals or groups need not coincide with those of the larger whole, nor is it always possible to so structure incentives and behavior rules as to channel their autonomous activities invariably into socially desirable directions. The more demanding the public interest—as determined by the political process—the greater the gap between these and the interests of particular groups or individuals, the least adequate the individuals' incentives from the standpoint of society, the greater the need to centralize functions to avoid subverting the public interest and social priorities. It is partly in these terms that one can explain much of the extreme centralization in communist economies. But the same causes operate elsewhere, too; for example, in private business corporations.

A closely related instance is the use of direct measures by central authorities to effect a quick and large-scale transfer of resources from one use to another, as in the case of the mobilization of men and productive capacity in wartime or for rapid industrialization under very adverse conditions. True, in some such cases—though not in all—the owners of the resources could be "bribed" to transfer them, but only at the price of a socially unacceptable redistribution of income and at the risk of setting off (or aggravating) an inflation.

Yet another reason for centralizing decisions relates to what the economist calls external economies and diseconomies. These are instances in which the full social benefits or costs of an activity do not or cannot enter into the individual firm's calculations simply because they are not "appropriable" by the firm. A private electric power company that builds a dam for power-generating purposes may thereby also diminish the risk of flood damage downstream, but nobody pays the company for the latter benefit and it does not enter into the company's calculations over whether to build the dam at all. On the other hand, a factory that pollutes a river may cause considerable damage downstream, but these social costs would find no reflection in its own profit and loss statement.[12] In the first case the power company may find it uneconomic from its own standpoint to build the dam, while the broader social calculus would favor it. A possible solution in this case would be to have some public authority build the dam. In the second case, the factory may not be justified from a social standpoint, although it may be profitable by itself. A good deal of centralization—through government regulation, taxation or subsidies, nationalization, or outright prohibition—is prompted precisely by such instances and aims to bring private and social costs or benefits closer together or to prohibit the practice.

Another frequent reason for the centralization of certain economic functions or decisions in a democratic society no less than in any other is the need to avoid socially disruptive or harmful, or politically unacceptable results that bargaining in the market place (or refusal to bargain by some party) may bring about. In this general class fall such activities of government in all democratic advanced countries as intervention in labor disputes and legal provisions for orderly procedure for their resolution, support of farm incomes, anti-monopoly legislation, and so forth. We shall return to these forms of government intervention in our discussion of the market economy in Chapter 5. Although the political procedures and administrative techniques may be different, totalitarian governments, including those in charge of command economies, also have to face the general problem of resolving conflicts between broad socio-economic groups (even if these groups may not openly organize to advance their interests, as they do in democracies).[13]

In no society or organization are the circumstances that prompt centralization or decentralization quite static. Conditions, values, problems change constantly, sometimes at an almost imperceptible pace, sometimes in large jumps. The issue is never finally resolved.

[12] External economies and diseconomies are sometimes called "neighborhood effects" or simply "externalities." The example of the dam is discussed at greater length by Otto Eckstein in *Public Finance* (Englewood Cliffs, N.J.: Prentice-Hall, 1964), this series, pp. 11-13. An extensive survey of external diseconomies caused by U.S. business will be found in K. William Kapp, *Social Costs of Business Enterprise* (Bombay-New York: Asia Publishing House, 1963). These diseconomies are no small matter. Kapp mentions (p. 89) a U.S. Public Health Service estimate that the total costs required for the elimination of water pollution would amount to $10.6 billion "over the next decade," slightly over half of which would have to be spent by private industry for the construction of waste treatment facilities. Other estimates run even higher; e.g., ". . . some pollution specialists claim an outlay of $70 billion to $100 billion may be required in the next few decades to raise the nation's waters to a desired standard of cleanliness" (*The Wall Street Journal*, April 15, 1965, p. 1). We shall be taking another look at externalities—from an institutional standpoint—on pp. 51-52.

[13] The term "incomes policy" is acquiring currency, especially in Western Europe, to describe the general policy or policies of the central government with regard to the relative shares of broad socio-economic groups in the national income.

Ideologies and "Isms"

CHAPTER THREE

An *ideology* is a set of ideas, more or less shared by a social group (e.g., nation or class), that (1) represents a certain picture of social reality, (2) sets up desirable values and goals for society to strive for (or preserve). We may not always be aware of it, but few of us are without a set of notions and ideas that in their totality form some kind of ideology. In any society there is a constant interaction among reality, ideology, and the socio-economic institutions (system).

Needless to say, ideologies do not fall from the sky. They arise in specific historical contexts, in response to definite circumstances and needs and in relation to other sets of ideas. But it would be an oversimplification to hold that they merely express the self-interests of individuals and groups, if only because such self-interest is not always easy to identify. Nor do ideologies remain stable; rather, they tend to evolve in response to changing circumstances, sometimes so imperceptibly that the process is not evident to contemporaries. An ideology that remains unbending in the face of a changed reality—i.e., a *dogma*—cannot hope to survive very long, and action based on it cannot hope to be successful in the long run. The durable ideologies are the flexible and adaptable ones, which often also means the less precise ones.

An *industrializing ideology*—an important phenomenon among the less industrialized countries in the modern world—typically sees highly developed industry (especially "heavy" industry) as the key to domestic prosperity and to national power and prestige in the world. It is frequently used to justify radical changes in society, to elicit political support and even heavy sacrifices for the sake of industrialization from the population, and to legitimize a given developmental strategy and a given politico-economic system. A very common key ingredient of such an ideology is *nationalism,* often coupled with fear or envy of powerful neighbors or colonial powers. Examples are Imperial Germany and Tsarist Russia before the First World War, and Japan before the First and Second World Wars, and dozens of underdeveloped countries today. Even present-day communism—which has become largely an extreme form of industrializing ideology nearly everywhere it is in power—is heavily suffused with nationalism. In systemic terms, as a rule, the more pronounced the quest for rapid industrialization and the more backward the initial conditions, the more is production stressed at the cost of equity and individual security, the higher the degree of centralization of political and social processes, the greater the role of the state, and the more extreme the economic (and political) means employed to attain and maintain rapid growth.[1]

Ours is an age of "isms": capitalism, socialism, communism, Marxism, fascism, Leninism, Titoism, revisionism, African Socialism, and so on *ad infinitum.* They stand for political movements, ideologies, doctrines, policies, economic and social systems, utopian dreams. Only too often they also serve as facile labels that do us dubious service. Their very proliferation attests to the growing inadequacy of most of the old labels to represent something definite, which only confirms the old truth that neither ideas nor events stand still.

Thus, it behooves us to avoid thinking in terms of discrete "grand alternatives," to try to escape from the "tyranny of the 'isms,' "[2] and to appreciate the great variety of actual—and even more so, potential—institutional patterns. Yet to recognize this much is not to dismiss entirely their analytical meaningfulness, or their historical importance. We therefore devote the rest

---

[1] A convenient, brief discussion of the major ideologies of American capitalism in the postwar era may be found in R. Joseph Monsen, Jr., *Modern American Capitalism: Ideologies and Issues* (Boston: Houghton Mifflin paperback, 1963). A more detailed treatment is in Francis X. Sutton, Seymour E. Harris, Carl Kaysen, and James Tobin, *The American Business Creed* (Cambridge: Harvard University Press, 1956; Schocken paperback, 1962).

Some remarks on the relevance of capitalism and socialism to underdeveloped countries will be found in Chapter 8 ("Conclusions"). Regarding industrializing ideologies see, for example, Alexander Gerschenkron, *Economic Backwardness in Historical Perspective* (Cambridge: Harvard University Press, 1962), especially Chapter 1. For the web of relations between ideology, "industrializing elites," industrial management, and labor in the process of industrialization see also the following books: Clark Kerr, John T. Dunlop, Frederick H. Harbison, and Charles A. Myers, *Industrialism and Industrial Man* (Cambridge: Harvard University Press, 1960; Galaxy paperback, 1964); and Reinhard Bendix, *Work and Authority in Industry* (New York: Wiley, 1956). The argument of Clark Kerr *et al.,* is conveniently summarized in their "Industrialism and World Society," *Harvard Business Review,* Vol. 39, No. 1 (January/February, 1961), pp. 113-126.

[2] These phrases belong to Robert A. Dahl and Charles E. Lindblom, respectively a political scientist and an economist, who in their important book on social systems and processes, *Politics, Economics, and Welfare* (New York: Harper paperback, 1953), especially Chapter I, take a strong position along these lines.

of this chapter to a brief survey of some of the most important "isms" as they bear on economic systems.

CAPITALISM

"Capitalism" is a word that we constantly use but rarely stop to define with any degree of precision. For present purposes let *capitalism* denote an economic system in which productive assets are predominantly privately owned and production is primarily for sale.[3] Advanced Western economies also contain smaller or larger publicly owned sectors; they are mixed economies, in the sense in which we have already used this term.

The private owner's object is to earn a handsome profit from the use of his productive assets. This much is obvious—and the profit motive, coupled with the institution of inheritance and bolstered by the law of contract, is the great engine of capitalism; indeed, the greatest source of economic drive in all history to date. But what is socially acceptable by way of profit-making in one epoch is not in the next. Laws and mores change. In the sixteenth century it was regarded as perfectly proper to seize on the high seas another country's treasure ships, which themselves may have been carrying precious metal that today we would regard as no better than looted or obtained through inhuman exploitation of native miners. Subsequent centuries, through most of the nineteenth, witnessed slave traffic and slave labor on a vast scale. And even as little as half a century ago, much business in this country was conducted with a disregard for the public, workers, investors, and natural resources that would be shocking and often illegal today. The progressive imposition of social—moral as well as legal—restraints on profit-making[4] need not mean an impairment of capitalism over the long run. On

[3] The second part of this definition is necessary in order to exclude subsistence economies, in which the means of production, albeit very simple, are usually also privately owned.

The beginnings of modern analysis of capitalism as a social and historical phenomenon lie primarily with Karl Marx and his associate Friedrich Engels, whose life spans covered nearly the whole nineteenth century. Their approach and conclusions, which we take up briefly later in this chapter, have profoundly influenced, whether positively or negatively, directly or indirectly, nearly all subsequent writings on capitalism. Among other writers of note we may mention two German social scientists, Werner Sombart and, again, Max Weber. (For an excellent summary of their views see Talcott Parsons, " 'Capitalism' in Recent German Literature," *The Journal of Political Economy*, Vol. XXXVI, No. 6 (1928), pp. 641-661, and Vol. XXXVII, No. 1 (1929), pp. 31-51. In his classic work, *The Theory of Economic Development* (Cambridge: Harvard University Press, 1934; original German edition in 1911) the Austrian economist, later Harvard Professor, Joseph A. Schumpeter, placed the innovative and creative functions of capitalism at the center of his analysis. In another famous book, *Capitalism, Socialism, and Democracy* (New York: Harper, 1942), published three decades later, Schumpeter saw a mature sluggish, corporate capitalism that was on the verge of evolving into socialism. A system of "countervailing power," of large economic power blocs in balance, is the main theme of John K. Galbraith's *American Capitalism: The Concept of Countervailing Power* (Cambridge: Houghton Mifflin, 1952). Of approximately the same vintage but less unorthodox in approach is David M. Wright's *Capitalism* (New York: McGraw-Hill, 1951; Chicago: Regnery paperback, 1962). A convenient list of many recent American works on U.S. capitalism may be found in the bibliography to Monsen's *Modern American Capitalism, cited.*

[4] We noted some in our discussion of private property, *supra*, p. 18. It is not intended to suggest here that the moral and ethical problems of private enterprise have been completely solved. Far from it.

the contrary, by adapting the limits of private profit-making to the (themselves evolving) standards of humanitarianism and justice, and by assimilating various other measures of social welfare, capitalism has tended to gain in popular acceptance precisely in those countries that have had the longest experience with it.

Private ownership, free enterprise, production for the market, profit-making—these are not only economic phenomena. They set the tone for all aspects of society and all sides of man's life and culture. Those who have studied the appearance and development of capitalism in historical perspective—great thinkers such as Adam Smith, Karl Marx, Werner Sombart, Max Weber, John A. Hobson, Thorstein Veblen, Joseph A. Schumpeter, and John M. Keynes—stressed the characteristic spirit, mores, values, and attitudes of the capitalist society, and contrasted it sharply in these regards with preceding historical eras.

Earlier Capitalism

As for capitalism's earlier stages, the aspects of its spirit that have been frequently stressed are enterprise, venturesomeness, acquisitiveness, competitiveness, and the urge to innovate. The dominant values that have characterized capitalism (especially in the Anglo-Saxon countries) are individualism, material progress, and political liberty. Writers such as Weber and Sombart stressed rationality as a characteristic attitude (or, to them, "spirit") of capitalism that distinguished it sharply from earlier eras. By "rationality" they meant the deliberate subjugation of means to definite ends, especially to the end of pecuniary gain, a careful weighing of alternatives, the keeping of systematic records, and, on the negative side, break with tradition, superstition, and magic.

The frequent view that the ideology of early capitalism was typically that of *laissez faire* [5]—no interference in economic activity by government, whose functions would be limited to that of a "night watchman"—i.e., a mere protector of life and property and (one should add) enforcer of contracts—is not correct. Even in Britain, the most advanced capitalist country for several centuries until the last quarter of the nineteenth century, the ideology of *laissez faire* prevailed for only a relatively short span of time; say, during the second half of the nineteenth century. Before that, in England as in most other countries in Europe, the prevailing doctrine was *mercantilism*—the doctrine that the state has the right and duty to both regulate and protect private enterprise, regarded as an instrument for the state's greater power and glory. Even in the heyday of individualistic capitalism in the United States—say, between the Civil War and the Great Depression—the dominant ideology was that of not pure but modified *laissez faire,* one which, on one hand, diluted free competition with tariff protection and large federal subsidies for railroad construction, and on the other hand increasingly accepted government

---

[5] Literally, "let them do"—i.e., leave business alone. The phrase was coined by French economists of the later part of the eighteenth century known as *physiocrats,* who opposed government interference with business.

regulation of public utilities and "trust busting." In Germany, France, Russia, and Japan—all relative latecomers to industrialization—*laissez faire* was regarded as a luxury that only the most advanced capitalist countries could afford. In these countries, under the impact of nationalist sentiments, active government protection and promotion of domestic private (and sometimes state-owned) industry were readily accepted and sought in the decades before the First World War. At the same time, government enforcement of competition found little favor, and the monopoly, the cartel, and the powerful bank became the dominant capitalist institutions on the Continent.

The growth of capitalism, and particularly of capitalist industrialization, meant also the creation of large working classes in the more advanced countries. Often crowded in miserable slums in the new cities that industry spawned, working long hours for low wages and under harsh and unhealthy conditions, deprived of the stabilizing institutions of the villages whence many of them came, and for decades left out of the orderly political processes— the workers of Europe [6] were at once indispensable to the success of capitalism and its greatest social and political problem throughout this earlier phase of industrial capitalism. It was for and among them, sparked by ideas of intellectuals often of middle-class origin, that radical ideologies and political movements, especially socialism, developed to challenge the capitalist order.

Contemporary Capitalism

Capitalism's prospects did not appear very bright on the whole immediately after the Second World War. True, it had been capitalism that brought about the remarkable advances and productivity and material well-being in the course of the nineteenth and early decades of the twentieth centuries. But capitalism was also associated in the minds of many with terrible wars, the business cycle culminating in the world depression of the thirties, great inequalities in income and wealth, colonialism, and much social tension. To communists, its end would inevitably arrive through revolution and class war, hastened by the alleged incapacity of capitalism to deal with its own problems. The great enhancement of Soviet power and prestige after the war, the communist takeovers in Eastern Europe and China, and the rise of large communist parties in some Western countries (notably Italy and France) made their prognosis that much more telling. Democratic socialists in the Western countries were looking forward to the peaceable demise of capitalism via the ballot box, and were much encouraged by the electoral victory of the Labor Party in Britain in 1945. Others who were neither revolutionaries nor radicals, as for instance Joseph Schumpeter [7] at Harvard, were predicting a slow but inevitable loss of vigor and enterprise on the part of the bureaucratized large capitalist firms and the consequent gradual transformation of capitalism into socialism.

Things did not work out this way. In the two decades following the war, capitalism not only proved its staying power but in addition exhibited greater dynamism and creative capacity than ever before, both in the advanced industrial countries and in a number of less-developed ones. In some countries—

[6] Thanks to its early establishment of political democracy, its very favorable population:resource ratio, its frontier of settlement, the ethnic multiplicity of its working class, and a number of other factors, the United States shared these conditions and problems to a much smaller extent, of course.

[7] *Capitalism, Socialism, and Democracy.*

especially in Western Germany, Italy, Austria, France, and above all, in Japan—the growth of production and the rise in average consumption levels have been remarkably rapid. At the same time, business fluctuations and unemployment have been minimized in the advanced capitalist countries (though less in the United States and Canada than elsewhere). However, it is not our purpose here to recount economic history; the interested reader is referred to Richard T. Gill's book in the present series [8] and to the many references therein. Some of the salient systemic properties of modern capitalism we shall be taking up in Chapter 4. Rather, at this point we shall cast a brief glance at the "ism" side of the subject; that is to say, at some of the basic institutional, ideological, and attitudinal differences between the capitalism that has obtained in the advanced countries since World War II and the earlier varieties.[9]

Perhaps the most significant feature of postwar capitalism has been the politico-economic equilibrium among, and mutual acceptance of, business (especially, big business), government, and organized labor in the advanced countries. In most cases, to this pattern of co-existing forces should be added two others: agriculture and small business, both impinging on the national economic picture as much through political channels as through strictly economic ones. Business has come to accept the active intervention of government in the economy for the sake of enhancing economic stability, promoting growth, reducing insecurity, and softening the economic inequities generated by the market place and exacerbated by inequalities in individuals' endowments or bargaining power. In some countries, private business has also acquiesced in the presence of substantial nationalized sectors and in active economic planning by the government. Furthermore, business has accepted collective bargaining with powerful organized labor as a regular and permanent arrangement. These attitudes, bolstered by the growing sense of professionalism on the part of management in large corporations, have been reflected (particularly in America) in the new "managerial ideology," which, without abandoning the profit objective, stresses management's responsibility to various elements within and without the corporation (employees, customers, suppliers, the general public, as well as the stockholders).[10]

On its part, labor has tended to accept the existing social order and to moderate its political goals. This has been to some extent true even in those countries, such as Italy and France, where a dominant segment of the labor movement has been under communist control ever since the war. This declining militancy of the various national labor movements has in turn contributed to the moderation of radical left-wing ideologies and the progressive

[8] *Economic Development: Past and Present* (Englewood Cliffs, N.J.: Prentice-Hall, 1963).

[9] For a good overview of these changes as regards the United States and Western Europe, see Calvin B. Hoover, *The Economy, Liberty, and the State* (New York: Twentieth Century Fund, 1959; also Anchor paperback, 1961), Chapters 7-9.

[10] Cf. Monsen, *op. cit.,* Sutton *et al., op. cit.,* and the essays by Robert L. Heilbroner, Earl F. Cheit, and Paul A. Samuelson in Cheit (ed.), *The Business Establishment* (New York: Wiley, 1964).

29

shift of the socialist parties toward the center of the political spectrum. In many advanced capitalist countries the conflict between capital and labor, though by no means extinguished, is no longer the paramount social problem it once was. Lately it has been rivaled by the problem of adjusting the less modern sectors, small-scale agriculture and small business, to the needs of a modern economy without undue human hardship or political instability.

ANTI-CAPITALIST "ISMS"

From the beginning, industrial capitalism induced a series of critical and hostile reactions which took the form of various radical ideologies and political movements, most of which fall under the very broad rubric of socialism. In turn, many (though far from all) of the socialist ideas and movements of the last hundred years have been the direct or indirect offspring of two towering intellectual and revolutionary figures of the nineteenth century, both Germans but long-time residents of England, Karl Marx (1818-1883) and his close collaborator Friedrich Engels (1820-1895). For over a century capitalism and socialism have been in continuous and close reciprocal relationship. For about half a century a third element, communism, interacted with the first two. In the process, all three have been substantially affected, though in different ways and to unequal degrees. The rest of this chapter takes up Marxism, communism, and socialism—their social and philosophical origins, evolution, and present state.[11]

Reactions to Early Industrialization

The negative features of early capitalist industrialization, which we have already briefly mentioned, produced several types of anti-capitalistic response. There were those among the educated classes—shocked with William Blake (1757-1827) by the desecration of "England's green and pleasant land," or of other countries, by the "dark, Satanic Mills"—who romanticized the past and who would have, if they could, stopped and reversed the historic process.[12] There were some among ordinary workers, like the English "Luddites" of 1811-1812, who gave vent to their misery by smashing the machines. There were others, usually among the more skilled workers, who tried to organize labor unions, often in the face of police repression as well as the hostility of employers. Lastly there were the "utopian socialists"—Frenchmen like Saint-Simon (1760-1825), Fourier (1772-1837), and Cabet (1788-1858), and the indefatigable Scottish industrialist Robert Owen (1771-1858)—who saw

[11] We have space here only for the briefest treatment. The interested reader is referred to Carl Landauer's extensive and thorough *European Socialism: A History of Ideas and Movements* (Berkeley: University of California Press, 1959), 2 vols., which contains a long bibliography in Volume II. *Socialism and American Life* (Princeton: Princeton University Press, 1952), edited by Donald D. Egbert and Stow Persons, may surprise the contemporary reader as it brings out the place of socialism in the history of this country. A most readable and at the same time scholarly history of socialist ideas up to 1917 is Edmund Wilson's *To the Finland Station* (New York: Doubleday, 1940; also in paperback).

[12] An excellent discussion of such "social-minded conservatives" of that era and of other responses to early capitalism will be found in Landauer, *op. cit.*, Chapter 1.

the root of social evil in the existing institutions, and especially in private property and selfishness; who drew up blueprints for a more perfect society, usually based on communistic or cooperative principles of work and distribution of income; and who (or whose followers) set up a good number of model and typically short-lived communities.[13]

MARX

Unlike the "utopians," Marx and Engels sought to discover the inexorable laws of history and of society, to delineate the inevitable future. Accordingly, they called their variety of socialism *scientific;* for the utopian socialists and their blueprints of ideal communities, Marx [14] had nothing but scorn.

His historical determinism was only one of many ways in which Marx was a product of his own era. His belief in the powers of reason and science as applied to man, for prediction as well as for analysis, and in the perfectibility of man, he derived from the Enlightenment of the preceding generations. His political economy stemmed largely from that of the English Classical School of the late eighteenth and early nineteenth centuries. His philosophy rested on German philosophy of the same period, especially on that of Hegel (1770-1831). His emphasis on class conflict was strongly colored by the experience of early industrial capitalism. His appreciation of the role of revolutions in history was greatly affected by the imprint left by the French Revolution of 1789 and by subsequent upheavals in Europe, especially those of 1848 and the Paris Commune of 1871.

Marx was a very prolific writer. *The Communist Manifesto,* written jointly with Engels on the eve of the revolutionary events of 1848, is one of the great political documents of all time.[15] His *magnum opus* is *Capital* (3 volumes, first published in 1867, 1885, and 1894), which presents an exhaustive analysis of the development and functioning of the capitalist economy. There are few aspects of philosophy or society that Marx did not address himself to, usually at great length. Marxism is an all-embracing world-view; it purports to explain and interpret all significant aspects of social life and thought on the basis of certain basic principles and laws, and likewise to predict the future of humanity.

[13] Many of these were in the United States, of which the two most famous were Owen's New Harmony (est. 1825) in Indiana and the Fourierist Brook Farm in Massachusetts during the 1840's.

[14] For the sake of brevity we shall henceforth refer to Marx alone, while always remembering Engels' close relation to him. Notice also the distinction between the adjectives *Marxian* and *Marxist.* "Marxian" pertains to Marx himself; "Marxist" pertains to "Marxism"—i.e., to everything that in some sense takes its origin from him and his ideas.

[15] There are many editions of this document in English. One with a very helpful introduction and annotations by Samuel H. Beer, and with important brief selections from other Marxian works, is published by Appleton-Century-Crofts (New York: 1955) in their Crofts Classics series.

THE MARXIAN THEORY
OF HISTORY

The Marxian theory of history belongs to the family of economic interpretations of history (hence, "historical *materialism*"). To Marx and his followers it is the economic facts of life ("the basis") that determine the nature of other aspects of society ("the superstructure," such as law, culture, religion, art, philosophy, and so forth) at any given epoch in history. More specifically, the decisive economic factor is the given period's *mode of production*. This somewhat vague notion encompasses both society's production capacity and its level of technology ("productive forces"), and the relation of various classes (landlords, capitalists, workers) to the production process ("production relations").[16] Depending on the mode of production, there is or is not *exploitation* in a given society, exploitation being the appropriation of the product of labor of some class or classes (slaves, serfs, workers) by others (slave owners, feudal lords, capitalists). The antagonism between classes is a central theme in the Marxist view of history: "The history of all hitherto existing society is the history of class struggle," Marx and Engels wrote in the *Communist Manifesto*.

According to Marx, all mankind sooner or later must pass through the same succession of six major historical stages: primitive (tribal) communism; slavery; feudalism; capitalism; socialism; and communism.[17] Under primitive communism, and again under socialism and full communism, the means of production are owned in common, and hence at these stages there is (in Marxian terms) no division into classes and no exploitation. In the three intermediate stages—slavery, feudalism, and capitalism—the means of production are owned or controlled by small segments of the population (the "exploiting classes"), with the majority of the population toiling for their benefit. Of course, when Marx and Engels were writing, there was yet no socialist society (let alone a communist one) in existence; but they were predicting its inevitable arrival, just as they were predicting that those societies that had not yet arrived at capitalism would of necessity get there in time.

Socialism and Full Communism

Although in their view both socialism and full communism are characterized by the absence of private property and other common features, Marx and his followers distinguish sharply between the two. (1) *Productivity:* Under socialism society is as yet unable to produce enough to meet all its material needs; under full communism it is able to do so, it has reached "abundance." [18]

---

[16] Indeed, in Marx, classes are *defined* in terms of their relation to production. By contrast, modern social science avoids a fixed definition of class and prefers to adapt it to the purpose of the given investigation.

[17] In the earlier Marxist writings, socialism and communism were generally regarded as two sub-stages—the "lower" and the "higher"—of the post-capitalist stage. Also, lately there is a tendency among non-Marxist scholars to refer to communism in this sense as "full communism" in order to distinguish it from the other meanings of the word (e.g., a political movement), a convention that we shall follow henceforth.

[18] But notice that "need" and "abundance" are very vague notions which have never been satisfactorily defined for this purpose in Marxist writings.

(2) *The nature of man as producer:* Under full communism, it is expected, work will be man's "second nature," he will work willingly, cheerfully, efficiently, and highly productively without requiring any direct incentive, such as a wage. Under socialism, however, man is not yet sufficiently reformed in this direction; he still requires material incentives to work enough and well. Hence the famous Marxian formula expressing the principles of income distribution in the two cases: under socialism, "from each according to his ability, to each according to his *labor*"; under full communism, "from each according to his ability, to each according to his *need.*" Since both scarcity and the need for individual incentive will disappear with the arrival of full communism, there will be no more use for money, prices, finance, and the like. These too will disappear under full communism, according to Marx. So will the state, for in Marx's view the function of the state is to support whatever exploiting class may be in power at a given time. No scarcity, no classes, no exploitation, no state.

Notice that the official Soviet ideology does not claim that the USSR has arrived at full communism yet. Rather, it claims to have arrived at socialism and to be building the *basis* of (full) communism.[19] We need not stop to consult our crystal ball as to whether it, or any other country, will ever arrive at full communism *in the Marxian sense.*[20] But we may remark that it is to Marx's great credit to have realized, over a century ago, that the progress of technology is pushing mankind toward ultimate abundance, and to have seriously posed the question of what society will be like when (we may add: and if) it gets there.

Marxian Historical Dynamic

Technology is the basic dynamic force in history, according to Marx. Each of the above-named historical stages corresponds to a technological level; hence their sequence and inevitability. Unlike many other stage-scheme builders—of whom there were a good number in the nineteenth century, especially among the so-called German Historical School of economists—Marx had a definite mechanism for transition from one stage to the next. As he saw it, the progress of technology builds up and develops the "productive forces" of a country. The institutions, however—the "production relations" in particular —for a while change little. At first, the production relations "correspond" to the productive forces; they enable the technology and capacity of the economy to produce rather fully. But with time, the production relations tend to lag more and more behind the development of productive forces; eventually, they become a hindrance to the full utilization of the latter. In the meantime, the

[19] For this reason it is not at all paradoxical (as is sometimes assumed) that the Soviet Union retains wages, other forms of individual material incentive, prices, money, etc. Many western socialists deny that socialism obtains in the Soviet Union and other communist countries, because for them socialism means primarily social justice and political freedom.

[20] Of course, it is possible to arrive at something different from what Marx envisaged and still call it full communism. There is a perceptible tendency in Soviet writings towards such redefinition.

development of productive forces gives rise also to a new class, which in time seizes power and refashions society's institutions to its own liking and needs —i.e., produces a new set of production relations that is again in harmony with the level of development of productive forces. But the advance of technology does not stop here; the process resumes anew, propelling society through another epoch of social tension, revolution, and the emergence of yet another historical stage—until finally socialism takes over from capitalism; the working class—the last in the historical succession of dominant classes—captures power, and through the further progress of technology *and* the reeducation of man leads society into full communism.

MARXIAN ANALYSIS
OF CAPITALISM

The capitalists' success necessarily creates a large working class— in Marxist language, a *proletariat*—which has no source of livelihood other than the sale of its own labor power.[21] With time, the inexorable working of economic forces causes the other classes effectively to disappear and society comes to consist of just two mutually hostile classes: the capitalists, who are the owners, managers, and employers of labor; and the propertyless proletariat. Under capitalism, the bourgeoisie controls the state—that is to say, the ultimate instruments of force and coercion which administer society for the bourgeoisie's benefit.

As we have mentioned, *Capital* is devoted to an extensive and incisive analysis of the economics of capitalism. A basic Marxian premise is the *labor theory of value,* which rests on the axiom that all economic value is produced by labor (and not by any other factors of production), and argues that all goods produced for the market ("commodities" in the Marxian terminology) tend to have prices which are proportional to their "socially necessary labor content." [22]

According to the Marxian view, labor power under capitalism is just another commodity. Hence, labor's wages conform to the same price-forming law as do prices of commodities in general; they are at the level which is just

---

21 Much Marxist terminology has a quaint ring to American ears. The *proletariat* and the *bourgeoisie* are the working and capitalist classes, respectively. *Proletarian, bourgeois* are the corresponding adjectives; as nouns, they designate individual members of the two classes.

22 Marx borrowed the labor theory of value from the English Classical School, especially David Ricardo (1772-1823), but he adapted it for his purposes—namely, to show the existence of exploitation under capitalism (see next paragraph in text) and the inevitability of its eventual doom. Notice that one must distinguish between (a) the source of value in a philosophical or metaphysical sense, in which case one can call it virtually anything to one's liking, and (b) value in the sense of relative price of a commodity (in relation to other commodities) as it in fact appears on the market in either the short or the long run, in which case one must refer to a positive theory of price formation (e.g., supply-and-demand), and (c) value in the normative sense—i.e., what should the value (price) of a given good be given certain over-all economic objectives and a certain mechanism of resource allocation in society. A modern "western" economist would say that prices would indeed tend to be formed in a capitalist market economy as the Marxian theory of value would have it if (1) labor were the only scarce factor of production and if (2) one considered only the long run. The first condition is unrealistic; the second, not exhaustive.

necessary for the "reproduction" of the labor force—i.e., for subsistence and bringing up the next generation of workers. (Marx postulated the existence of continuous unemployment which would prevent wages from being bid up above the subsistence level.) But under capitalism, technology is so far advanced that the average worker can produce far above his and his family's own subsistence needs. This excess, "surplus value," is appropriated by the capitalist, from which the latter derives his own consumption needs and (most important) the savings to finance further "accumulations" (investment). A part of the surplus value also goes to other property-owning classes—as interest to financiers and as rent to the owners of land and other natural resources. At the same time, the appropriation of the surplus value by capitalists constitutes his "exploitation" of the workers.

The dynamics of capitalism occupies the center of the Marxian economic analysis. Though, at first, capitalism constitutes an unprecedented engine of material progress, eventually it *must* run into greater and greater difficulties and cause growing misery to the vast majority of those living under it. Ownership of capital—and with it, by definition, all power—become more and more concentrated with time; the polarization of society is aggravated. In the course of their constant search for profits, capitalists over-invest, which leads to a long-run decline in the rate of profit, and also to sharp periodic declines, the so-called "crises." [23] And meanwhile, the proletariat becomes poorer and poorer (the so-called "immiseration theory").[24] Revolutionary feelings among the workers mount, until at some propitious moment a successful proletarian revolution overthrows capitalism.

To the cause of such a revolution Marx devoted a large part of his life. He died in 1883; Engels, in 1895. As the nineteenth century gave way to the twentieth, Marxist parties had become by far the most important radical parties in the world, except in the English-speaking countries. And at the same turn of the century there began a process of repeated fissioning of the Marxist movement, so that today the historical progeny of Marx and Engels include such militant parties and ideologies as Maoism and Castroism, and such moderate ones—in some cases all but rejecting their Marxist heritage —as the social democratic parties in Western Europe.

An Appraisal

It is easy to find fault with Marx. Though his theory of history has been quite influential, most Western historians today reject its brand of economic determinism and its rigid stage scheme. His economic theory was primitive even for his own day, but he must be given credit for pioneering in the theory

[23] A careful survey of the Marxian theory of crises and some of its implications by a leading American Marxist scholar will be found in Paul M. Sweezy, *The Theory of Capitalist Development: Principles of Marxian Political Economy* (New York: Oxford University Press, 1942), Chapters 8-12.

[24] There has been considerable debate whether Marx meant that the proletariat becomes only *relatively* poorer, or also *absolutely* so. The point is of historical and theoretical importance, although for lack of space we have no choice except to by-pass it here.

of business cycles. Of all the modern social sciences it is perhaps sociology that owes most—directly and indirectly—to Marx as the first modern political sociologist.[25]

Nor did his prognoses fare better. True, as he expected, industrialism grew and spread on the face of the globe, and technology continued its rapid advance. But industrial society did not become progressively more polarized into the wealthy few and the proletarian mass. Nor did the workers become progressively poorer. On the contrary, in the advanced countries, the material levels of living of the masses rose decisively, a large and generally conservative white-collar class came to play an increasingly important role in social and political life, and the revolutionary fervor of the working class has been on the wane. Marxist (communist) regimes did gain power in about a dozen countries, but almost invariably under conditions that were the very opposite of those anticipated by Marx. Withal, for better or worse, no single individual in the past hundred years has had a greater influence on history than this impecunious researcher in the British Museum, writer of ponderous German tomes little read in his own day, and contentious, ill-tempered leader of a small revolutionary sect.

LENINISM

Vladimir Lenin (1870-1924), founder of the Bolshevik (Communist) party of Russia and of the Communist International, leader of the successful Bolshevik Revolution in 1917, and founder of the Soviet state, was much more than a fervent follower of Marx. He was above all an innovator, adapting Marxism to new conditions and pushing its theory and practice in new directions, the importance of which for our century's history cannot be overrated.

First, drawing on a long Russian tradition of revolutionary action, Lenin developed the notion of a professional, conspiratorial party, internally authoritarian and highly disciplined, as the instrument of revolution.[26]

Second, Lenin refused to admit the necessity of waiting for the maturation of capitalism in order to carry out a successful socialist revolution, as Marx's more orthodox followers insisted. According to them—and to Marx himself—the establishment of socialism in a backward, agrarian country was an absurdity. But Lenin saw that the revolutionary potential of a poor, disaffected, land-hungry peasantry could be harnessed for its own ends by a party speaking in the name of the working class. The political chaos, social upheaval, economic difficulties, and revulsion against war that characterized Russia in 1917, after three disastrous years of participation in the First World War, gave the Bolsheviks their opportunity.

[25] See Schumpeter, *Capitalism, Socialism, and Democracy,* Chapters 1-4, for an engaging discussion of Marx as prophet and scholar.
[26] More correctly, Lenin elaborated and grafted onto the Marxist world-view the theory of professional conspiratorial activity that originated with Russian revolutionaries in earlier decades. The written material on Lenin and Leninism is very large. A comprehensive analysis is Alfred G. Meyer's *Leninism* (Cambridge: Harvard University Press, 1957).

The Leninist formula of seizure of power with its four basic ingredients —determined leadership by a small revolutionary elite, economic backwardness, a disaffected peasantry, and war against an invader or a colonial power —worked again during and immediately after the Second World War in Yugoslavia, China, and Vietnam. Indeed, this non-Marxian way is virtually the only way in which communists have gained power in Russia or elsewhere, apart from being brought to power by dint of Soviet military force.[27] Yet the weakness of the Leninist formula is inseparable from its success. When power is seized by a highly authoritarian small party whose ideology is not shared at the time of the take-over by the bulk of the population, when especially the social class that is the instrument of victory—the peasantry—has aspirations very different from those of the communist leaders, when the new regime feels that it must engage as soon as possible in feverish industrialization at virtually any cost, and when it regards itself hostile to all or most of the world at large—under these conditions, as the history of communist regimes amply shows, political democracy has three strikes against it, and the door is open to the severest political repression and terror.

Today, Lenin is a highly revered figure among all communists despite the profound differences among them. Indeed, the greater the ideological conflict among the various factions of communists, the greater the tendency for each to build up Lenin's image while claiming fidelity to his ideas. As a result, "Leninism" today stands for whatever orthodoxy the given brand of communism may wish to uphold.

STALINISM

Lenin died only six years after the Bolshevik Revolution and before the Soviet economy had completed its reconstruction from the ravages and strains of the First World War and the Civil War. The USSR as we know it today—economically, socially, and politically—is largely the creation of Joseph Stalin (1879-1953), who seized power after several years of bitter struggle against other communist leaders and ruled the country for the next quarter of a century, until his death, as the most absolute of modern dictators. Today, "Stalinism" is a virtual synonym for the highest degree of ruthless and bloody totalitarianism.[28] And, unlike Marxism or even Leninism, it is not so much a coherent system of ideas as a way of doing things.

[27] For lack of space, we abstract here from the special case of Castro's Cuba.
[28] Totalitarianism has been defined in several ways. One may think of it as a dictatorial regime which, through a single mass party and police intimidation, seeks to exercise *total* control over society and to maximally impose its ideology on the mind and the spirit of its subjects.

DEMOCRATIC SOCIALISM [29]

If the authoritarian, more-or-less revolutionary communist parties of the world represent one major branch that grew from the Marxist trunk, the moderate, reformist, democratic socialist parties of Western Europe and some other advanced countries of the non-communist world represent the other. It would be difficult to imagine more dissimilar political cousins than, say, the Social Democratic party of Sweden, on the one hand, and the Chinese Communist party, on the other. Present-day communist regimes are primarily political vehicles for the ruthless industrialization of backward countries, a job that was reserved for capitalism by Marx, while one of democratic socialism's chief functions at the present juncture is to enhance the effectiveness and distribute widely the benefits of what are otherwise essentially advanced capitalist economies. It is hard to tell which of the two is farther removed from the original Marxism.

Democratic socialism—or, as it sometimes is called, "social democracy" —has had many ideological sources. The most important of these, especially on the European continent, was Marxism, or, more exactly, its revisionist stream. The revisionists of that era argued that Marx's prognoses regarding capitalism were not coming true. Capitalism was not heading for a certain collapse, nor were the workers becoming more miserable (rather, the contrary). On the other hand, with the growth in its numbers, the working class in the advanced countries was now in a position to play a large and increasing role in orderly political life, and with time even to seize power by parliamentary means. The revisionist position was violently opposed by the revolutionary-inclined Marxists, who saw in it an ideological heresy and a betrayal of the proletarian cause. But it did find a strong appeal, especially in Germany, among many workers, trade union leaders, and intellectuals who either subscribed to the revisionist analysis of capitalism or preferred gradual advance to violent revolution.

Another important ideological source of democratic socialism has been the ethical teaching of the various Christian (especially Protestant) religions. (In Catholic countries socialism has had a strong anti-clerical aspect.) Christian Socialists, as such socialists came to be known, saw in the individualism, acquisitiveness, inequality, and other features of the capitalist order the very opposite of the good society implicit in Christian teachings. Such, for instance, has been the major philosophical basis of socialism in Britain. The mass support for socialism, where it has existed on a mass basis, has nearly always been provided by a strong labor movement allied to the Socialist party, and to some extent (particularly in Scandinavia) by a broad consumer cooperative movement. Yet the political and ideological leadership of democratic socialism—as for that matter usually also of revolutionary communism— typically has been provided by relatively small groups of intellectuals, of whom perhaps the most famous was the gradualist, non-Marxist Fabian Society of England (organized in 1882).

[29] The reader is again referred to the works by Landauer and Egbert-Persons cited in footnote 11, this chapter.

There is no space here to relate the history of democratic socialism—especially its bitter, and all too often desperate and tragic, battles against communism, fascism, and Nazism from the nineteen twenties on. Nor shall we dwell on the record of socialism in the United States, where it has played a significant role in the history of the labor movement but was unable to establish itself durably owing to specific American economic, cultural, and political factors.[30] Rather, we shall take a brief look at the present-day complexion and ideology of social democracy, particularly as it has lately emerged in advanced countries other than the United States, and especially in Western Europe.

To do so we first have to take a backward glance at the period between the two World Wars. During those two fateful decades the European Social Democratic (S.D.) parties were still overwhelmingly proletarian in their class-consciousness, voting strength, and policy orientation. Insofar as their ideologies originally derived from Marx—which would embrace virtually all the S.D. movements on the Continent—their basic commitment to Marxism (albeit to the revisionist version) was still very strong. Working-class solidarity and the fundamental conflict with capitalism were the twin pillars of their political programs, which of course aimed at the eventual establishment of socialism by democratic means. Capitalism was condemned for a long list of social evils: economic inequality, the poverty of the working class, unemployment, the worker's alienation from the production process, the distortion of social and cultural values, crime, war, and so forth. The values stressed by the S.D. parties were political freedom and democracy, individual security, and the elimination of economic inequalities of all kinds. It is these values, of course, that involved them in struggles with totalitarian movements and regimes (which in turn often regarded social democracy as their greatest enemy) and, during the thirties, against the Great Depression.

As the S.D. parties saw it at the time, the basic instrument for the achievement of their domestic goals was to be the nationalization of at least the most important industries or sectors of the economy. If the prime evil was private property, then the basic solution lay in taking the most important means of production out of private hands, though with compensation to the former owners, and their transfer to public ownership, preferably of course under a S.D. government. Planning, especially for full employment and a more egalitarian distribution of income, received some attention in socialist writings of the time, as did the possible use of the market economy under socialism. But these discussions remained largely on the theoretical plane, for few socialist parties came to power in the interwar period or retained power long enough or under sufficiently favorable conditions to translate their programs into action.[31]

[30] See Egbert and Persons, *op. cit.;* also Walter Galenson, "Why the American Labor Movement is not Socialist," *The American Review,* Vol. I, No. 2 (Winter, 1961), pp. 1-19.

[31] A conspicuous exception is Sweden, where the Social Democratic party came to power in 1932, at the bottom of the depression, and successfully put through a series of employment-raising and social welfare measures.

After the Second World War, and especially after Western Europe's economic recovery, the S.D. parties came to be faced with a distinctly new situation which was soon to lead to major ideological and programatic re-thinking and revising. Within each country, the chief elements in the new situation were the economic success of capitalism (or at least of a mixed economy) and major shifts in the social structure. Thus, economic growth has been very rapid in many advanced countries (e.g., West Germany, France, Italy, Austria) and, by old standards, appreciable even among the laggards (e.g., Belgium, United Kingdom, Scandinavian countries), consumption levels have risen correspondingly, and (equally significantly) economic fluctuations and unemployment have been minimal. The share of white-collar employment in total employment increased rapidly, and even the blue-collar labor force, thanks to rising incomes, increasingly tended to absorb middle-class aspiration. Class-consciousness tended to be blunted. A strictly working-class appeal thus carried little promise of future electoral successes. Moreover, the same socio-economic trends rendered Marxist analysis of capitalism and Marxist attitudes increasingly irrelevant. On the other hand, even conservative govern-ments went in for extensive social welfare programs and sometimes (espe-cially in France) for far-reaching economic planning, thus taking some of the wind out of the socialists' sails.[32]

By the late fifties and early sixties many of the continental S.D. parties had dropped even nominal ideological allegiance to Marx. The greatest policy change has been the virtual abandonment of opposition to private property *per se* and of the goal of nationalization. This came about through a greater awareness of the danger of perverting socialist ideals through the excessive bureaucratization and enhancement of governmental power that may follow nationalization. Also instrumental were the instructive experience of Eastern Europe, where these negative phenomena occurred on a large scale; the dis-illusionment with the nationalization programs in Western Europe immedi-ately after the war, which often created as many problems as they solved; the realization that under modern conditions the control of industry, whether for private or social ends, is more important than ownership; and a more sophis-ticated appreciation of the possibilities for exercising such controls without outright public ownership. And nationalization has also tended to lose in voter appeal. The new S.D. position therefore became: private ownership as a rule, public ownership only where necessary, and maximum reliance on the mar-ket economy, the latter, to be sure, supplemented by conscious governmental steering and planning and by extensive welfare measures.[33]

[32] As the New Deal did to the Socialist party in the United States.

[33] At this point it is necessary to stress that the above description pertains to the general tendency among European (and similar) socialist parties. Within almost every such party there has been a "left wing" faction that has opposed this tendency and has fought for more militant, working-class oriented, anticapitalist, and perhaps more tra-ditionally Marxist policies. In Italy—reflecting that country's semi-developed nature—the large Socialist party has taken the "left" position, even collaborating electorally with the even more powerful Italian Communist party until the late fifties, while the "right wing" view has been represented by the much smaller Social Democratic party. Elo-quent defense of *right wing* socialist view may be found in the writings of the prominent British Laborite C. A. R. Crosland, such as *The Future of Socialism* (London: Jonathan Cape, 1957) and *The Conservative Enemy* (New York: Schocken, 1962). A brief but forceful statement of a British "left" view is Edward H. Carr, *The New Society* (Lon-don: Macmillan, 1951; Boston: Beacon paperback, 1957).

These developments have confronted democratic socialism with a dilemma. As an American observer has well put it: ". . . if it means the replacement of the mixed economy by total public ownership of the means of production and distribution, it ceases to be democratic, and that, if it means no more than a changed mix in the mixed economy, it ceases to be socialistic." [34] As we have seen, the actual trend has been toward the latter alternative, which at times may appear to be little more than a kind of "me-too-ism" with regard to the non-socialist parties (which return the compliment by committing themselves in turn to the welfare state, high employment, and other traditional socialist goals). It has been suggested, consequently, that the S.D. parties will direct their efforts primarily toward more comprehensive economic planning (though within a market economy), equality of opportunity (as in education), and the safeguarding of political democracy against its enemies, from both the left and the right.[35]

[34] Arthur Schlesinger, Jr., in a review of Crosland's *The Conservative Enemy* in *The New York Review of Books,* Vol. I, No. 2 (1963), p. 6.
[35] Cf. Landauer, *op. cit.,* Vol. II, Chapter 47.

The Capitalist

Market Economy

CHAPTER FOUR

ANGLIA:
THE PERFECT-COMPETITION MODEL

It often helps us to gain insight into a complex phenomenon by first investigating a relatively simple, if unrealistic, one. We shall therefore begin the present chapter by outlining and analyzing a very simple model of the perfectly competitive market economy. This model—which we dub *Anglia* in honor of the English (but also Scottish) classical and neo-classical economists who put it on the theorist's map—has had an active life in economic-theory textbooks and other academic works, bears the venerable patina of long-time pedagogic usage, and has shaped our capitalist ideologies. It is entirely imaginary; no such real economy exists, has existed, or is likely to exist. But this should not embarrass us so long as we remember its fictitious nature.

In Anglia, all resources are privately owned. Firms are managed by owner-entrepreneurs who aim to maximize profits. Households seek to maximize incomes. No firm, let alone a household, is large enough to affect in the market the prices of things that it sells and buys—i.e., there is perfect competition. On the government's part, *laissez faire* is observed; but property is protected, contracts are enforced, weights and measures are set, money is provided, and (moderate) taxes are collected. Firms have freedom of enterprise and households have freedom of household choice.[1]

42

[1] For the meaning of these terms see p. 8.

Prices move freely. The market mechanism coordinates production and distributes incomes. Labor, unorganized, and other factors of production receive the rewards that the market concedes them.

Invoking the criteria of Chapter 1, how may we appraise Anglia? First, the criterion of plenty: We cannot tell from the model itself how affluent Anglia's citizens are, but we may surmise that they are probably not very affluent by modern standards if their economy is so "backward"—so devoid of large-scale production and pressing socio-economic problems—as to preserve perfect competition and avoid government intervention in the operation of the market mechanism. On the other hand, economic theory tells us that a perfectly competitive economy with profit maximization (and abstracting now from such complications as external economies and diseconomies) tends to attain *static* efficiency.[2] We need not fear lack of entrepreneurial drive, for owners are at once profit-maximizers and their own managers. Also, because assets are managed by their private owners, there will be a tendency for physical capital to be well cared for. *Dynamic* efficiency is something else again, depending as it does largely on the adoption and diffusion of technical innovations. On this score we need not be too sanguine. Although private property and competition provide the incentive for innovating, the organizational and financial resources to conduct large-scale modern-style research, development, and promotion of new products may not exist in Anglia. To be sure, there may still be a good deal of the more "old-fashioned" kind of inventing and innovating. On the other hand, a good deal of innovating would also create many disequilibria in the economy, establish more or less monopolistic advantages for some firms, and thus undermine our assumption of perfect competition. Equally uncertain is the verdict on growth, which depends on dynamic efficiency and, even more, on the rate of investment in the national product. The last may or may not be relatively high, depending on the economy's saving propensity. Yet with profits held down by competition to a "normal" level, this most important source of savings may not be very large. Nor can we say much about economic stability, which would depend in part on the nature of the monetary system (which we here by-pass); but the dispersion of spending and saving decisions among many decision units makes economic fluctuations not unlikely.

As for economic freedoms, they exist in our model by assumption. Household sovereignty (in the sense defined in Chapter 1) also probably obtains to a high degree, for reasons that the reader is invited to confirm for himself. Regarding the distribution of wealth, nothing very definite can be said on the basis of the bare model. A market economy with the institutions of private property and inheritance creates the conditions for amassing wealth and retaining it within families over generations. In our model this tendency remains (by assumption) unchecked by any deliberate wealth or income redistributive action on the part of the state. On the other hand (also by assumption), monopoly is absent and economic opportunities are unconstrained

[2] We defined static efficiency on p. 7. See also Robert Dorfman, *Price Theory*, this series, Chapter 6.

by government, so that there are no artificial barriers to the replacement of old wealth by new.

We must distinguish clearly between the "real" result, the efficient allocation of resources, and the particular *institutions* which tend to bring it about, which in this case are those of Anglia. It is possible that another set of institutions—i.e., another model of an economic system—will bring about the same result, static efficiency. (Though not necessarily the same bill of goods. As we have just seen, the bill of goods depends on the pattern of final demand, which in turn depends on the distribution of income and wealth among households, which may well be different under a different set of institutions.) Thus, in Chapter 7 we shall look at a model of a *socialist* market economy, which in theory also yields full static efficiency. Moreover, it is conceivable, though in the near future not very likely, that all resource-allocating decisions in the economy will be entrusted to a battery of electronic computers properly programmed to achieve static efficiency and holding the requisite data in their "memories." The computers would presumably issue detailed production orders to individual firms, though households may still retain both sovereignty and freedom of consumer choice. In this case we would have a kind of command economy with what has been called "perfect computation," [3] achieving the same resource-allocating—though probably not social and political—result as does the automatic but non-automated market mechanism under perfect competition. In this imaginary case the electronic computing center—machines, mathematicians, and (hopefully) economists—is the functional equivalent of a social process.

On the other hand, the market mechanism as such must not be thought of as always producing static efficiency. It will do so, theoretically speaking, only under Anglia's very special conditions, which are not satisfied in real economies, sometimes not even remotely. For instance, as we shall see in a moment, perfect competition is hardly the rule in advanced capitalist countries. We must therefore conclude that real—especially, advanced—economies operate at levels of static efficiency that are considerably short of perfect. This is regrettable but not entirely tragic. Full static efficiency is only one of several desiderata that we expect of the economy, and to a significant extent we have to sacrifice the former in order to do better on other scores, such as higher growth, stability, higher over-all productivity, equity in income distribution, and so forth, as we saw in Chapter 1. Ours would be an unhappy world if society's only purpose in the economic domain were the attainment of perfect allocative efficiency.

THE ADVANCED
CAPITALIST ECONOMY

We are now ready to turn to the modern, advanced, capitalist (or mixed) economy. In the remainder of the present chapter we shall enumerate some of the ways in which it contrasts with the uncomplicated world

[3] The phrase is Wiles'; see P. J. D. Wiles, *The Political Economy of Communism* (Cambridge: Harvard University Press, 1962), Chapter 10. This is an imaginative and stimulating book on alternative institutions and systems, capitalist as well as communist.

of Anglia, as well as the sources and nature of some of its major problems. The next chapter will be devoted to a discussion of the ways in which the modern, advanced, industrial, capitalist (or mixed) economy is subjected to conscious social regulation and control.[4]

How, then, does such an economy differ from Anglia? Perhaps the most fundamental difference is that firms are often big, not uniformly small as in Anglia, or tend to band together into large associations of various kinds to advance their common interests by economic or political means. This bigness in the production sector is the result of an historical process, conditioned as it was by nineteenth- and twentieth-century technological advances which at times entailed large economies of scale, by the natural tendency of private firms to grow as large as is profitable (and sometimes even larger), and the desire to limit competition through merger or some looser sellers' association. To be sure, even in the United States, there is still a great deal of small business, but it is the giant corporation that dominates the economic scene.[5] Other economic interests, faced with big business and big government, have tended to band together to form labor unions, farmers' associations, and even consumer organizations to enhance their own bargaining power vis-à-vis the giants. And government at all its levels, faced with (or acting for) the many agglomerated economic problems of industrialized society, has long since abandoned any professions of *laissez faire* even in those countries (United Kingdom, Netherlands) where it can be said to have been entertained in the earlier capitalist era. In France, Italy, the United Kingdom, and several other advanced industrial countries of Western Europe, the national government participates importantly in the production sector by means of nationalized enterprises.[6] Along with bigness, and because of it, modern society in the West, let alone in the Communist East, tends to be bureaucratized—in large corporations, government departments, labor unions, educational institutions, and other sizeable organizations. And bureaucratization means hierarchical

[4] In addition to the United States, Canada, and most countries of Western Europe —all of these falling into the North Atlantic group—the advanced capitalist (or mixed) countries are usually deemed to include Australia, New Zealand, Japan, and the Union of South Africa, the last with reference to its white minority. Any such classification is somewhat arbitrary.

[5] In the United States, in the early sixties, the 500 largest (by sales) industrial corporations accounted for some 55 per cent of the aggregate sales and of the total employment in manufacturing and mining. In 1963, the 500th had sales of $86 million; the largest, General Motors, had sales of $16.5 billion, held assets of $10.8 billion, earned net profits after taxes of $1.6 billion, and employed 640,000 persons. In that year, the 50 largest (all but one having sales of over $1 billion) accounted for just half the sales of the 500, 51 per cent of the assets, 59 per cent of the net profit, and 46 per cent of the employees. (Sources: *The Fortune Directory: The 500 Largest U.S. Industrial Corporations,* [etc.] (annual) and various U.S. statistical publications.)

[6] For example, in France (in 1957) public enterprises generated 10 per cent of the national income, employed 7 per cent of the labor force, and accounted for 25 per cent of all gross investment in the country. In Italy, public enterprises mine all the iron ore and extract nearly all the natural gas, generate nearly all the electric power (since 1963, when the industry was nationalized), accomplish most of the shipbuilding, produce about half the steel, and play important roles in many other industries and sectors. For further discussion of nationalization, see Chapter 5.

relations, managers and the managed, and a "web of rules" in society as a whole and within every organization.

1. Private property, ownership, and management. In the millions of small businesses, ownership and management still either reside in the same person(s) or are in any case closely connected, but this is not so in large "private" corporations. In the latter, the nominal ownership rests with thousands—sometimes hundreds of thousands—of dispersed shareholders, while management is in the hands of a small group which may own only a very tiny proportion of the corporation's outstanding shares of stock. Thus, in the large corporation, the business form that dominates our economic landscape, ownership and control are separated. Ownership does not carry with it managerial responsibility, while those who bear such responsibility are not significant beneficiaries of the firm's successes or take much pecuniary risk in its failures. Often, management is virtually self-perpetuating, since no group of outsiders, even stockholders, can hope to dislodge it easily. This independence of corporate management has been bolstered by the growing tendency of corporations to finance the expansion of their assets from internal sources, i.e., depreciation reserves and retained profits.[7] Under these circumstances, what motivates managers to hold down costs, operate efficiently, earn high profits for the firm, innovate, expand the business in response to favorable expectations, or for that matter even to prevent dissipation and undermaintenance of capital assets? How much of a difference is there between such management in private corporations and its counterpart in nationalized companies? In fact, in nationalized companies management may be much more amenable to control on the part of the nominal owner—i.e., the state. All in all, we might expect big business to be sluggish, unenterprising, undynamic, inefficient. Yet we know that, by and large, even in the giant private corporations, this is not so. Management in advanced capitalist countries does the things that are expected of it by society and on the whole does them fairly well. As we have already pointed out, capitalism on both sides of the North Atlantic has been unusually dynamic during the post World War II era.

These and related problems have been studied a good deal since the problem of separation of ownership from control was first systematically posed in the early thirties,[8] yet there is no convincing simple explanation for the "proper" behavior of corporate management. Many factors seem to be at play, such as the incentive effect of the bonuses that executives derive from successful operation (but to what extent are these bonuses in effect self-awarded?), the general understanding by managers that profits are a yardstick by which the rest of the business community takes their measure, the cultural forces in an advanced industrial society which place high value on such things as

[7] In the early sixties, in the U.S., the share of internal sources was about 60 per cent.

[8] The pioneering classic work was Adolf A. Berle, Jr., and Gardner C. Means, *The Modern Corporation and Private Property* (New York: Macmillan, 1933). For a latter-day return to the same subject by one of its authors, see Adolf A. Berle, *Power Without Property* (New York: Harcourt, Brace & World paperback, 1959). On this related issue, see also Edward S. Mason (ed.), *The Corporation in Modern Society* (Cambridge: Harvard University Press, 1959).

efficiency and growth, and the feeling of professionalism among managerial personnel, which carries with it a sense of social responsibility and of pride in a job well done. But wouldn't all or most of these factors be operative under public ownership ("socialism") as well? They probably would, provided managers were given a high degree of autonomy (which is not the case in Soviet-type economies, so that these do not provide a fair answer to our question). Indeed, the experience of nationalized enterprises in Western Europe suggests that, under comparable conditions, management is approximately equally effective and efficient in both sectors.

2. *Profit and other goals.* However, it would be naive of us to assume that the exclusive goal of advanced capitalist countries is profit maximization. To be sure, the large private corporation, like any private firm, must avoid consistent losses or it will go out of business. It may, however, merely aim at some "satisfactory" rate of profit—it may be "satisficing" rather than maximizing. Or it may strive to maintain some "traditional" share of the industry's market; or it may attempt to maximize the rate of growth of its sales, because this rather than profits may be the chief "success indicator" in the business community.[9] Withal, it may still be trying for higher profits, though how hard it tries may depend on many things, such as whether the firm is young and aggressive or the opposite; what the norms of behavior in this regard in the given country or industry are; how pressing are the immediate or anticipated needs for financial liquidity, and whether management is not apprehensive that high profits will invite pressure from labor unions for higher wages or the attention of the Anti-trust Division of the U.S. Department of Justice. Lastly, as A. A. Berle has repeatedly stressed,[10] the large corporation may feel a sense of responsibility to all with whom it deals directly and to the public at large.

In sum, profit-*making* still seems to be a very important goal for the large capitalist firm. But it is not the same as simple profit-maximizing, as economic theorists often assume; hence the theoretical conclusions that we may draw regarding efficiency and the like in the advanced economy must also be surrounded with appropriate qualifications.[11]

3. There is no reason to assume that the behavior of *households* or the freedom of choice available to them is significantly different in an advanced capitalist economy than in Anglia, apart from enjoying a higher standard of living and partaking more or less of the welfare state.

4. *Competition.* Clearly, with all its big business and government intervention (not always to promote competition), the advanced capitalist economy is hardly *perfectly* competitive. Indeed, the preservation of at least a "workable" degree of competition in industries and sectors dominated by big business—or the regulation or nationalization of those industries in which competition would be unlikely or uneconomical—is one of its major politico-

[9] This thesis has been forcefully argued and explored by Robin Marris in *The Economic Theory of "Managerial" Capitalism* (London: Macmillan, 1964).

[10] For instance, in his *The 20th Century Capitalist Revolution* (New York: Harcourt, Brace & World paperback, 1954).

[11] Cf. Dorfman, *op. cit.,* pp. 38-40.

economic problems. For *some* significant degree of competition—not necessarily perfect—is essential in a market economy to limit market power (which is translatable into political power as well), to safeguard reasonable efficiency of operation, and to ensure that the profit-making is a socially beneficial motive force and not merely a charge on the national income.

Altogether, the economy as we know it seems to be quite competitive, even if far from perfectly so. Often the competition focuses not on price but on product quality, terms of sale, delivery conditions, and other non-price dimensions. There seems to be considerable agreement among specialists that the American economy (to mention one) has not on the whole suffered any substantial reduction in competitiveness, at least in the product markets, over the past thirty or forty years.[12] Two developments that have contributed to maintaining the intensity of competition since World War II are: (1) rapid technical progress, which may create patent-protected monopolies, but also increases the range of mutually substitutable products and thus enhances competition among them; and (2) the reduction in scope and "height" of barriers to international trade, which has tended to intensify competition across national frontiers.

5. Prices perform the same two functions as in Anglia: They supply information on which economic decisions are based, and they are a direct or indirect source of individual and corporate net income. However, in industries that are not perfectly competitive, sellers (or buyers) have power to affect prices. In these cases, which are important, covering, for instance, a large part of manufacturing, prices are also often not very flexible; they do not respond quickly to changes in demand or supply. In the regulated industries prices are usually set by governmental commissions and are therefore quite inflexible in the short run. In some respects price inflexibility is a good thing. It helps general price stability, makes economic decisions based on these prices less uncertain, and may cause less fluctuation in the incomes of certain groups than if prices were very flexible. But since price flexibility is also an important factor in the adjustment process that reallocates resources in response to changing demand and supply conditions, the lack of it in a modern market economy may interfere with reasonable speedy adjustment to disturbances or to changes in social objectives.

This problem becomes especially pronounced when prices are held at certain maximum or minimum levels by government action. Examples are, respectively, the farm price supports in the United States (and, in some form or other, many other countries) and general price controls at times of serious inflationary pressure, as in wartime. The common purpose behind this and similar measures is a perfectly legitimate—and often socially and politically desirable—one of protecting (or raising) the incomes of certain groups within the country that would be adversely affected by the unhampered operation of the market mechanism (more on this problem presently). But in doing so, these measures may also impair the performance of the other major function of prices, that of facilitating resource reallocation in the economy. In the case of general price controls, the price:cost ratio may become so unfavorable while at the same time, owing to the inflationary developments, there is such an excess of money in the public's hands, that production and work incentives

[12] Cf. Joe S. Bain, *Industrial Organization* (New York: Wiley, 1959), Chapter 6.

may be seriously damaged. Whether the socio-political effects of tampering with prices outweigh the economic costs to society as a whole and to individual groups is of course in itself a political question.

An interesting problem arises when the price is paid not by the consumer of the good but by a third party. The best known instance in the United States is the sponsoring of radio and television programs. The consumer enjoys the programs free—though he may be paying a price in terms of having to listen to or watch advertising ("commercials") that he may rather forgo, and possibly in terms of the quality and nature of the programs made available to him. The sponsor pays for the program and therefore usually decides, or at least influences, the content; he is obviously interested in maximizing the number of listeners or viewers so as to maximize exposure to his commercials. This situation, it has been often charged, leads to pitching the programs' appeal to a mass level, ignoring minority interests and tastes, and deleting controversial material. On the other hand, a way (e.g., "pay-TV") that would sell the service directly to the individual consumer, who may be willing to pay for the less conventional and more controversial programs, would presumably create the demand for such programs and would elicit their supply. An analogy can be drawn with books and journals. Since the consumers pay for them directly, they tend to be available in the greatest variety, though even here pressure from advertisers may seriously affect the content of journals heavily dependent on advertising, as mass-circulation journals are. We may mention in conclusion that the problem discussed in this paragraph is attributable not so much to the market mechanism as to the perversion of the role of prices where the final consumer does not pay for the good himself.

STRENGTHS AND DEFECTS

By and large, the market mechanism in the advanced economy operates remarkably well in automatically equating demand and supply for particular goods under normal conditions. Given effective demand, supply comes forth quite rapidly. The market mechanism can also be, and frequently has been, a powerful engine of innovation and progress.

Since it is a decentralized process, the market mechanism disperses economic power—though it may at the same time have the offsetting effect of helping to agglomerate power through the promotion of monopoly and the accumulation of private wealth. As we have already seen, the intensity of competition and freedom of economic opportunity play an important role in this connection. The market economy disperses not only power but also decision-making, responsibility, and initiative—which is desirable from the standpoint of the viability of democratic institutions. It also localizes ordinary business conflicts, settles them in the market place, and keeps them from migrating up to the higher levels of the political structure, as would be inevitable in a hierarchically organized economy. (On the other hand, it also **49** encourages the formation of pressure groups to bargain for economic advantages in the political arena where it cannot be obtained in the market place.)

The market mechanism's very impersonality, often and at times justly criticized, has its positive side. The market respects economic worth from whatever direction it may come, and thereby tends to provide—not always, to be sure—economic opportunities where they might otherwise be barred by social discrimination.

Yet with all its advantages and virtues, the capitalist (or mixed) market economy has a good number of faults and gives rise to enough problems to keep thousands of economists, lawyers, politicians, and legislators, as well as cranks and crackpots, busy trying to solve them. Which failures are caused by the fact that the advanced capitalist economy is a decentralized (market) economy? that its producers are primarily after pecuniary profit? that the means of production are typically privately owned? Analyzing the problem this way we may, at times, arrive at surprising answers.

The Market and Equity

Being impersonal, even blind to non-pecuniary considerations, the market mechanism pays little heed to distributive justice. It lavishes favors on the movie star and the professional athlete, allows the lucky property owner to reap windfall gains, but deprives of opportunities or suddenly impoverishes others through no fault of their own. Clearly, no modern society can leave income distribution to the market alone, not only out of feelings of solidarity with and compassion for the poor, but also because in a democracy (and even to some extent in a dictatorship) the adversely affected groups—not necessarily poor—are likely to bring political pressure on the government at some level to redress the social balance [13] in their favor. It is more difficult to do justice to groups of underprivileged citizens who, for various reasons, are politically powerless to command the attention of society, as we have learned in connection with the current "War on Poverty" in the U.S.A.—though it is not entirely impossible, as the same fact testifies.

Faults of Decentralization

Effective as a market economy is in balancing demand and supply in individual product markets, it is much less dependable with regard to macroeconomic balance. In other words, it has a pronounced tendency to fluctuate in the over-all level of economic activity and in general level of prices. It also has a tendency toward unbalance in one specific market, the market for labor; thus, in the United States between 1954 and 1964, despite relatively prosperous times otherwise, unemployment as a proportion of the civilian labor force (annual figures) never fell below 4 per cent and stood below 5 per cent in only three years. In short, unless vigorously counteracted, the market economy has a definite bias toward instability and less than full employment.[14]

The fundamental reason is its decentralized nature. The many millions of economic units—firms, households, governmental entities on all levels—make their spending and saving decisions autonomously and without direct

[13] As a politician once put it: "Those farms may be marginal, but the voters on them aren't."

50

[14] These aspects of the market economy are investigated in Charles L. Schultze, *National Income Analysis,* this series.

coordination. However, in the aggregate the separate decisions tend to have cumulative effects and to generate waves of favorable or unfavorable expectations regarding the future. The result can be, and often has been, boom or bust, prosperity or depression, inflation or deflation—unless appropriate stabilizing measures are successfully taken by the government (of which more in the next chapter).

A closely related cause of malfunctioning of the market economy arises from uncertainty regarding the future as it is seen by the individual firm. What will future prices and costs be? What technological advances will occur? What will be the state of business one, two, or five years hence? Should one risk a large investment in a new plant or in promoting a product? Each firm acting on its own may wish to observe a margin of safety, the cumulative effect of which is to hold back innovation and investment, dampen technical progress, reduce the rate of growth, and increase unemployment in the whole economy. Thus, not only is each firm justified in its caution, but the tone is set for further pessimism.

Depressions, unemployment, inflation, sluggish growth—these are obviously among the most serious problems an economy has to face. In the past, these ills have all but wiped modern capitalism off the face of the earth. They have been at the center of the socialist critique of private enterprise. Fundamentally, they stem from the decentralized and uncoordinated nature of decision-making in the market economy rather than from private ownership of means of production. They would exist as well in a socialist market economy in the absence of deliberate appropriate measures by the government. The crux therefore lies in the socio-political and ideological climate. Would such a climate permit or, on the contrary, resist and prevent public authorities from taking adequate stabilizing and confidence-inducing measures? The socialist argument has traditionally been that powerful private property interests in a capitalist society would prevent government intervention even for stabilizing purposes, and historically there has been much evidence to support this view. But, as we have already noticed in preceding chapters, lately there has been a considerable shift toward greater pragmatism in the prevailing ideology of modern capitalism on this score. Once hostile to resolute stabilizing measures by the government, the climate of opinion in the North Atlantic countries now tends to accept the idea, and even to expect it.

We have already had occasion to hint that the problem of externalities is basically caused by the decentralization of decisions (or their imperfect centralization) rather than by the capitalist nature of business activity or by profit-making as such. The problem arises because some of the benefit that the firm performs for society does not accrue to its own benefit (say, profit), and some of the damage it does to society is not a charge on its own costs. Thus, the firm is led not to do enough in the former direction and to do too much in the latter direction. In both cases, society loses. "Benefit" and "cost" to the firm relate to the particular objective that the firm pursues. If the firm's objective is profit, then benefit to it means more profit and cost means less profit. It seems unlikely that a realistic alternative objective in lieu of profit—

51

say, maximizing sales value—would reduce the scope and magnitude of external economies and diseconomies.[15] Thus, the problem of externalities seems to be just as pronounced in the Soviet Union as in any capitalist country, although Soviet firms (and their superior entities) are neither privately owned nor are they primarily profit-oriented, and even enjoy little autonomy except —ironically—to disregard many of the "classic" externalities.[16]

Faults of Profit-Making

Indeed, it is difficult to devise a generalized objective for the individual firm that would be socially more rational than profit-making. With appropriate prices, profit—as the difference between gross value produced and cost incurred—is the best measure of the firm's net contribution to the national income, whether under capitalism or under socialism, and therefore the best criterion for its autonomous action.[17] (We must distinguish here between profit-*making* and profit-*taking*. Who pockets the profit is something else again.) This much is now being slowly realized even by Soviet and other East European economists after decades of painful experience (see Chapter 6).

A major social rationale of profit as an automatic regulating instrument is that its simultaneous pursuit by all firms will be largely self-defeating—i.e., that competition will prevent excessive profits while pushing production of individual goods to levels consistent with (or at least approximating) over-all allocative efficiency. Needless to say, the individual producer takes a different view. He *likes* "excessive" profits and regards competition within his own industry with less than joy. There is nothing wrong with this. On the contrary, the very strength of the capitalist market economy lies in that it harnesses for social ends such a powerful motive force as the universal desire for economic self-betterment. It is therefore as illogical as it is unrealistic to expect people to eschew profits out of social consciousness, so long as they do not transgress the limits of law and accepted ethical standards. But it is society's function to ensure that profits serve a constructive function and that the profit motive propels activity into socially desirable directions rather than the opposite. In the American tradition this has meant that competition—an automatic and effective profit-restraining social device—is encouraged where feasible; and industries in which it is not feasible, because it would be too wasteful ("natural monopolies"), or for other reasons, are publicly regulated or controlled.[18]

[15] An independent (or autonomous) firm must have (or be assigned) a fairly clear-cut objective, such as profit, to enable it to make its decisions rationally (and, if it is a nationalized firm, to allow its performance to be impartially appraised). And while the firm is not thereby absolved from acting responsibly vis-à-vis society, it cannot be expected to take into account the effect of its actions on all third parties lest either it be paralyzed by the magnitude of the task or renounce its independence or autonomy.

[16] Pollution, deforestation, urban congestion, soil erosion, and similar products of industrialization and economic growth are all serious problems in the USSR. At fault is not only the neglect of external diseconomies by Soviet firms but also neglect of these problems by the regime and the planners in pursuit of hasty industrialization. The parallel with the United States several generations ago is striking despite the great difference in economic systems.

[17] The theoretically sophisticated will immediately realize that, externalities apart, "appropriate prices" are those which (a) define the demand-supply equilibrium, and (b) are equal to marginal cost, and that this is the situation with perfect competition at equilibrium.

[18] See Richard Caves, *American Industry; Structure, Conduct, Performance,* this series, *passim;* and Bain, *op. cit., passim.*

Nonetheless, even under reasonably competitive conditions some serious problems are caused or accentuated by profit-making. The most common of these is the defrauding or deception of the buyer by the seller. This is done in so many ways, crude or subtle, and takes so many forms, and is such a well-known phenomenon, that it requires no more than mere mention here. Deception or fraud can be checked by competition among sellers if there is a good chance of the buyer's discovering it and shifting his patronage to a more honest seller; indeed, this is the main reason why there is not much more of it than there is. Otherwise, competition only forces the more scrupulous to "fall in line" with the less scrupulous sellers in order to survive the competitive struggle. Because of his economic weakness and relative ignorance, the individual consumer is a more likely victim of deception and fraud than the buying firm. Government action—in the form of requirements to disclose package contents or product ingredients, standardizing nomenclature and product specifications (e.g., the U.S. Pharmacopoeia), enforcement of quality and purity standards, disclosure of true terms of sale, such as financing charges, etc.,—is called for, though it rarely reaches far enough because of producers' opposition. Other ways of combating deception and fraud are through "consumer unions," which test products and publicize their findings, or through consumer cooperatives,[19] which attempt to safeguard consumers' interests at the distributing and producing stages.

Another but related problem is that of excessive expenditure on advertising and other means of attracting consumer demand to a given product. There is no space in this context to discuss this complex matter in any detail.[20] We may mention, however, that (strictly speaking) neither excessive advertising nor consumer deception is as much a phenomenon of capitalism as of the profit-oriented market economy in general. There is no reason to believe that profit-oriented *socialist* firms would desist from these practices much more readily than do capitalist firms, in the absence of restraints on the part of public authorities or of countervailing pressure on the part of organized consumers. The reason is that the seller wants to increase profits (or, possibly, just sales); it does not seem to matter whether the profits benefit the owner-manager, or the corporation as such but not directly its executive, or even the socialist state.[21]

Faults of Private Ownership in Production

Yet this is not to absolve private ownership as such from certain important faults of its own. One of them is that the unit of ownership may be too small. A classic example is the oil and gas industry. Here, the fact that

[19] Consumer cooperatives may have various rationales: ideological (mainly anticapitalist, as with the important European consumer-cooperative movements), consumer education, enhancement of bargaining power vis-à-vis suppliers, and compensation for inadequate resource mobility. On the last point, if resources were mobile enough, private enterprise would presumably provide the economically justified services that cooperatives supply to their members.

[20] Again the reader is referred to Caves, *op. cit.*, esp. p. 102.

[21] Deception and defrauding of the consumer are widespread in the Soviet economy, where firms are not profit-oriented but are production-maximizers; see pp. 85-86.

a single underground deposit of oil or gas is owned by many owners of surface lots of land, each of whom fears that his share in the deposit may be lost to a neighbor unless he acts swiftly to extract it, leads to an uneconomically large number of wells, excessively rapid extraction, and perhaps the loss of some of the fuel underground. Another example pertains to the fragmentation of urban land-holding among very many owners with the result that it may be difficult to assemble a sufficiently large unit of land for an otherwise economical project, say, a large apartment house. There are of course ways of by-passing these obstacles for some purposes. In the petroleum industry, the rate of extraction from a given well is regulated by law in many states (though the same device may be used to protect the interests of the resource owners at the expense of consumers), which, however, does not restrain the drilling of too many wells and may even encourage it.[22] In cities, large "urban renewal" projects are undertaken by public authorities which resort to the privilege of eminent domain to assemble ample land areas.

Another defect is that the private owner may have too short a "time horizon"—i.e., he may discount the distant future more heavily than society as a whole would. This "after-me-the-deluge" attitude has caused much predatory exploitation of land, mineral resources, forests, and the like, especially in the earlier period of this country's westward expansion and industrialization when natural resources seemed to be inexhaustible. At times, the result was literally the deluge, as when deforestation impaired surface water retention and increased flood hazard. As a result, very costly soil reclamation, reforestation, and flood-control measures have to be undertaken by society, not to mention the irreparable losses of natural resources which have to be endured.

In a capitalist economy, private enrichment has a social function; it is the incentive for productive activity. To discourage it unduly is to undermine the economic order. But because it is difficult to distinguish in practice between enrichment that is the result of productive activity and that which is not, the latter tends to get the same legal protection and social sanction as does the former. From the social standpoint this is wasteful; some consider it unjust as well. For instance, the value of urban land appreciates as the city grows; landowners thus reap windfall gains without any productive contribution on their part.[23] Many other examples could be cited.

But perhaps the main difficulties that ensue from private ownership in the capitalist economy are of a different order. Thus, it creates powerful vested interests that are at times hard to control and regulate by democratic processes even if the general welfare would seem so to require; e.g., the tribute collected by the domestic silver-mining interests from the U.S. Treasury for

[22] A good, brief statement and analysis of the petroleum problem will be found in Bain, *op. cit.,* pp. 582-589 and 628. See also K. William Kapp, *Social Costs of Business Enterprise* (Bombay-New York: Asia Publishing House, 1963), pp. 148-152.

[23] We are referring here to the value of the land as such, not to man-made improvements. Of course, land can fall in value as well as appreciate. The most eloquent condemnation of "unearned" income from the appreciation of urban land is Henry George's *Progress and Poverty,* first published in 1879 and still a classic. His proposal for the socialization of land ownership, the income from which would constitute the only form of government revenue (the "single tax"), at one time received much attention but is not regarded by economists as the panacea for social ills that George and his zealous followers assumed it to be.

the better part of a century, or the opposition of local propertied interests to purely local improvements for fear of raising the property-tax rate. Perhaps as important but more elusive is the impact of the prevalence of private ownership on outlooks and attitudes. One result may be a subtle confusion of ends and means. Calvin Coolidge is reputed to have said: "The business of America is business." It is not, of course, in any ultimate sense. Private business is mainly a means to a more fundamental end, the material well-being and the general welfare of this and future generations. Private property, private enterprise, the profit motive—these are powerful social instruments for the achievement of society's goals. They are delicate instruments in that their effectiveness rests on confidence and trust. But they are still primarily means, not ends.

Furthermore, a private enterprise economy tends to bias production in favor of goods sold in the market ("private goods") and against public services, as has been forcefully argued by John Kenneth Galbraith, among others.[24] To begin with, public services are provided by government, and government tends to be suspect. Second, such services have to be financed by taxes, which are a burden to bear. Third, private goods are aggressively promoted by their producers; public services are more often than not apologetically defended.

[24] *The Affluent Society* (Cambridge: Houghton Mifflin, 1958), pp. 132ff. and 309ff. The book is an eloquent critique of present-day thinking and policies on the problems of the contemporary American economy.

Planning and Control

in Capitalist Market Economies

CHAPTER FIVE

PLANNING AND CONTROL

Attempts to shape or guide the economy through the prohibition or encouragement of trade, public works, and price and wage controls go back to the dawn of history and have continued through the ages.[1] But it has been in the last generation—owing to the Great Depression of the thirties, the Second World War, and the many pressing problems of the postwar world—that the role of government in economic life increased greatly everywhere in the world and growing attention came to be given, even outside the communist countries, to systematic and coordinated control over the national economy and its growth. Concurrently with these developments and closely related to them, there has been a marked advance in economics, which has brought a better understanding of the causes of business fluctuations, new insights into the growth process, new tools of analysis (especially mathematical), and a large body of writings on the planning, controlling, and "steering" of the economy.[2]

By control we mean the purposeful, deliberate shaping of

[1] With regard to the nineteenth and twentieth centuries see, for instance, Hugh G. J. Aitken (ed.), *The State and Economic Growth* (New York: Social Science Research Council, 1959).

[2] Very important also has been the almost simultaneous development of the digital electronic computer, which has made possible fast handling of large amounts of data for research, testing of economic theories, and for actual planning.

economic phenomena by public authority in the most general sense. It includes the concept of *planning,* the difference between the two being that planning carries a greater connotation of being rational (in the sense of being strictly subordinated to some definite goals), systematic, and of operating largely with quantitative variables. It is also the more accepted term when a longer period is in question.

Planning should not be confused with socialism, if by the latter term we mean widespread ownership of the means of production by the state or other public authorities. While a socialist economy almost certainly is also likely to be a planned one, planning in the broad sense in which we understand it does not necessarily call for nationalization of industry. Even less does it necessarily call for interference with freedom of enterprise or the freedom of the household. There can be and are very different kinds of planning with very different implications for democratic values. Some kinds, such as the Soviet variety, are clearly opposed to democratic values and to freedom of enterprise. Other kinds are quite compatible with them.[3] Regulation of aggregate demand by means of monetary and fiscal policy in order to maintain economic stability at high employment levels ("macro-economic planning"; see below, this chapter); promotion of certain socially desirable programs (e.g., urban renewal, area redevelopment, education); protection against some kinds of economic insecurity—all such measures rather than restricting economic freedom, go a long way toward enlarging the opportunities for private business and for consumers. This is the kind of planning that has been pursued by the recent national administrations in the United States, even if in this country we usually avoid the word because of its negative ideological and semantic connotations when applied to the federal government.[4]

Essential Elements of Planning

All planning worthy of the name displays the following elements or aspects.[5]

1. Purpose. By definition, planning must be directed toward the attainment of some objective (aim, goal, target), though it may be quite vague (e.g., full employment). The way in which the objective is determined depends on the polity's processes.

2. Authority. Since planning is deliberate activity, someone must initiate and undertake it. And since it operates by affecting the behavior of economic agents, its measures must be backed up by authority. In the case of governmental planning, the authority is of course political. Moreover, a distinction typically is made between the authority that sets the goals, ap-

[3] Thus, Eugene V. Rostow, *Planning for Freedom* (New Haven: Yale University Press paperback, 1959), speaks of "liberal planning" for this reason.

[4] But even in the United States the word "planning" carries a pejorative connotation only in reference to the federal level of activity. Business corporations, cities, counties, and even states freely admit that they engage in "planning" without fear of opprobrium. Because "planning" carries a pejorative sense in some contexts, the word "programming" is occasionally preferred.

[5] For a brief treatment of the formal aspects of planning see Jan Tinbergen, *Central Planning* (New Haven: Yale University Press paperback, 1964).

proves the plan or control measures, and enforces them, and the technical and administrative staff(s) that draw up the plans and observe their execution. The latter generally act only in an advisory capacity to the authorities, although in practice they may wield a great deal of influence because of their technical expertise and control of information.

3. *Level and scope.* The aims of planning and the authority behind it to a large extent determine the level of the planning activity—local, state, national, international—and its scope; i.e., whether it embraces all or nearly all of the given political unit's economy, or any particular industry, or a certain region. Business firms also plan.

4. *Time period.* During which period will the plan be in operation? Often there is a hierarchy of time periods—say, a general ten-year plan and detailed annual plans deriving from it.

5. *Estimate of the present and forecast.* The very intention to plan implies the perception of some existing or anticipated problem and is therefore to some extent always preceded by an estimate of the present situation and a forecast of future conditions that will obtain in the absence of a plan. The decision to plan may be followed by a much more thorough appraisal of the present or prospects for the future. Plans should be distinguished from forecasts or projections. While they necessarily rest on some estimate of the future, plans aim to affect deliberately the course of events and not merely to foresee them.

6. *Economic model.* All planning presupposes some idea of the relations among the relevant economic variables, some kind of economic model in the planner's minds. For instance, if the purpose of the plan is to eliminate a deficit in the balance of payments and so to stop a dangerous outflow of gold, it is essential to know the significant factors that affect the balance of payments directly and indirectly before corrective measures can be effectively taken. Often, the model is only implicit in the planner's actions. But the more sophisticated economic plans are based on explicit models, which in turn rest on economic theories.

Both the theories and the models may be couched in mathematical terms. Thus, a planning model may consist of a matrix (table) depicting the flows of goods and factors of production among the economy's sectors and industries. An input-output model would be an example; it could tell us what changes in flows and production will be called for by anticipated or desired changes in other outputs. Alternatively, the mathematical model might be an *econometric* one consisting of a set—perhaps several dozen—equations, linking a large number of variables (e.g., the price level, the wage level, rate of investment, level of consumption, level of income) and certain constants.

7. *Variables and instruments.* In any economic model that explicitly or implicitly underlies planning, there are two kinds of variables. First, there are those variables that planning seeks to bring to certain desired (target) levels or magnitudes, often called *target variables.* For instance, suppose it is desired to bring the outflow of gold down to zero or to maintain prices at a given level or to achieve a certain annual average rate of growth of national product. Sometimes the targets can be attained by a direct order; e.g., the conversion of the domestic currency into gold may be stopped by decree and thus the gold outflow may be halted, or price controls may be enacted to keep prices

at the existing level. However, these are extraordinary measures. More commonly, the government will manipulate some other variables, often called *instrument variables,* in order to affect the target variables indirectly. Thus, in order to stem the outflow of gold, the authorities may raise the domestic structure of interest rates, which will tend to keep domestic capital at home and attract foreign capital. The instrument variable is the structure of interest rates, and the explicit or implicit economic model is one that relates international capital movements to changes in interest rates. The range of instrument variables available to the authorities depends on the constitutional legal provisions, the nature of the economy, custom, and so forth. We shall return to consider instrument variables presently.

8. *Methodology and procedure.* The drawing up of an economic plan at whatever level is a complicated and time-consuming procedure. The timing of the work, the methodology employed, the procedures for putting together the plan document—these can vary widely. They will depend in large part on the aims of the plan, the nature of the underlying model, the available instruments, and of course many political and cultural variables.

9. *Enforcement and execution.* Some instruments are easy to handle, such as those that give away something for nothing (welfare payments, production subsidies, above-equilibrium prices, tax rebates). Others—taxes, price and wage controls, exchange controls—require much more elaborate enforcement because they may seek to compel people to act against their wishes or interests. Sound planning requires that the course of plan execution be closely watched for possible revision of policies if the effects diverge from the expected ones.

Types of Planning

A distinction often is made between *macro-economic* and *micro-economic* planning (or control). As the name suggests (*macro-* means "large" in Greek), macro-economic control or planning concerns itself with the economy as a whole and its major components or sectors. Its goals (target variables) are such as full employment, a certain rate of over-all growth, stability of both production and prices, and equilibrium in the balance of payments. Macro-economic planning does not concern itself, as a rule, with what happens to individual prices so long as the general price level remains constant, nor at what rates individual industries are growing so long as over-all growth is satisfactory. Being unconcerned with detail, macro-economic planning tends not to affect individual firms or even industries *directly,* though it very much affects them indirectly. Hence, it enlists less intense attention on the part of individual interest groups, which may be both an advantage and a disadvantage for its launching and success.

Micro-economic control or planning (*micro-* = small) aims at affecting an individual industry, sector, distinct region, or even firm (if it is large and important enough). In the United States, not only the federal government but all levels of government engage in micro-economic control. The purposes are many; the examples are innumerable. Among its purposes, one may mention

59

preservation or enhancement of defense potential (by protecting the watch-making industry against foreign competition, and by subsidizing such industries as shipbuilding and shipping) and natural resource conservation (as in the discussed case of petroleum, see p. 53). While most of us will agree that there arise quite a few situations when micro-economic planning is desirable in the public interest, there is inevitable controversy regarding individual policies and their instruments. And since in specific instances it is likely to be advocated most by those who are to gain most from it, it constantly tests the distinction between public welfare and the mere furtherance of private interests.[6]

Instruments

Control or planning represent a centralization of decisions and activities in the market economy.[7] In seeking to accomplish its aims, public policy in a market economy may either work through and with the market mechanism, or it may work against it, thwart its operation, or substitute something else for it. Instruments that work with and through the market mechanism are sometimes called *indirect controls* because they reach at their targets indirectly. Those that ignore or thwart the market by reaching for their targets directly are known as *direct controls*.

Direct Controls

Direct controls either prohibit economic acts or attempt to force them. Instances are many even in the United States where the general ideological opposition to them is stronger than in most other advanced, democratic countries. *Negative direct controls,* those that are prohibitive, include such measures as an embargo on trade with enemy countries, acreage limitations in the case of price-supported agricultural commodities, proscription of trade in narcotics or of importation of sugar above the annual quota, and so forth. The historical arch-example on the national scale was, of course, Prohibition in the twenties. Negative direct controls are especially numerous on the state and local levels in connection with zoning regulations (which forbid various kinds of construction or business activity in given urban districts), safety and sanitary codes, licensing, and so forth. To this category also belong (maximum) price and wage controls, though these are quite rare in the United States other than in wartime or as applied to regulated public utilities. Price control is often accompanied by rationing so that the limited supply of the given good(s) is more in accord with equity or social priorities.

The common economic feature of negative direct controls is that they cause disequilibrium in particular markets by restraining the adjustment of either supply or prices in the face of excess demand. This causes problems, not so much because some of the demand remains unsatisfied, which after all is usually one of the purposes, but because it invites evasion, black markets, contempt for the law, and costly enforcement. Moreover, price control causes

---

[6] Gerhard Colm, "Economic Planning in the United States," *Weltwirtschaftliches Archiv,* Vol. 92, No. 1 (1964), pp. 31-56, is a convenient survey. For another basic distinction—between indicative and imperative planning, see p. 69.

[7] See pp. 20 ff., *supra.*

wrong signals to be communicated to both sellers and buyers regarding the true scarcity of the good(s), thus distorting the operation of the market mechanism, as we already have mentioned.

Instances of *positive direct controls,* which require certain economic acts (other than taxpaying) of otherwise independent or autonomous entities, are also quite numerous, even in the United States. They range from the requirement that public utilities serve all legitimate customers, through federal and state anti-discrimination and industrial relations legislation, to the various local safety and health codes. Two major instances are compulsory education and compulsory military service. All these examples (with the exception of public utilities), however, tend to affect production as such only marginally, because in a market economy, and a democratic one at that, forcing firms by means of the government's police power into lines of production against their will tends to be both ineffective and politically unpopular. It is economically and politically often wiser to "bribe" them instead—i.e., to use indirect controls.

Indirect Controls

As we have indicated, indirect controls work with and through the market mechanism. They do so generally in one of two ways: by enlarging or contracting over-all purchasing power, or by making particular activities more profitable or less profitable. Often, both effects occur simultaneously, as when more favorable terms on government-financed housing at once stimulate the construction industry and, by expanding the volume of loans for the purpose, also enlarge the total purchasing power within the economy.

Stabilization policy, the major part of macro-economic planning, naturally depends heavily on instruments that influence over-all purchasing power. This is not the place to discuss either the policy or the instruments. Suffice it to remind ourselves that the most important instruments are (a) fiscal—i.e., the size of the government budget and the net budget surplus (or deficit), which directly affect private incomes; and (b) monetary policy, which manipulates the cost and availability of credit and thereby influences the actual volume of credit (and, hence, money) in the economy.[8] Macro-economic planning also can utilize *selective* credit controls, as in the housing example mentioned in the preceding paragraph.

Selective indirect controls are of course the main tools of micro-economic planning, and the toolbox available to government is large indeed—tariffs; taxes of all kinds; subsidies,[9] the terms and repayment provisions of credit for

[8] Yet another significant, though as yet not commonly used, stabilization instrument was developed in Sweden (see p. 68). This is the freezing and unfreezing of firms' internal liquid funds, the so-called investment reserves, in order to utilize private investment better for countercyclical purposes. With internal sources playing the dominant role in corporation finance in many advanced countries, this instrument is likely to receive more attention in the future.

[9] A useful compendium is U.S. Congress, Joint Economic Committee, *Subsidy and Subsidy-Effect Programs of the U.S. Government* (Washington, D.C.: Government Printing Office, 1965).

special purposes; matching or outright grants; support (i.e., above-equilibrium) prices, of which the U.S. farm price support program is among the most famous (or infamous, depending on one's view); minimum wage and overtime pay laws; and so forth.

Indirect controls have the important advantages of impersonality on the economic plane and of being compatible with the regular market mechanism. In effect, often they announce the rules of the game and let the market take over from there. (In the case of support prices, the government must of course be prepared to absorb the surpluses that the high prices bring forth.) The fact that indirect controls "distort" resource allocation or income distribution is not necessarily a convincing objection. Their purpose, after all, *is* to alter these things in order to achieve goals that the uncontrolled market will presumably not achieve by itself. Nonetheless, indirect controls *may be* objectionable for one of these reasons: the goal may be objectionable (we may not wish to stimulate family farming or private home ownership); the goal may be acceptable but the means may be regarded as inferior (it may be better to pay each farmer a capital lump sum in government bonds in exchange for terminating farm price supports); the indirect control is only a by-product of a measure imposed for another purpose, such as fiscal revenue, which nevertheless may be inhibiting some economic activity.

A major disadvantage of all selective controls, direct and indirect, is that they invite the pressure of special interests on all levels and against all branches of government. But in a market economy indirect controls are extremely advantageous, because they work through and not against the market mechanism, generally do not create disequilibria in individual markets, and are often more impersonal. Psychologically and politically, they have the great virtue of preserving the economic agent's freedom of choice while affecting the data on which alternatives are appraised. By contrast, direct controls are a form of coercion. Why then are direct controls used at all? Two answers suggest themselves: (a) when public interest calls for the complete cessation or unexceptionable pursuit of an activity that may not be stopped by taxing (trading with the enemy, distribution of narcotics) or sufficiently encouraged by "bribing" (compulsory education); (b) when resources have to be mobilized and redeployed so rapidly and in such a volume that "bribing" would not only create income inequities but would start or aggravate an inflationary spiral. The obvious example is the wartime economy, but many developing countries trying to advance as rapidly as possible find themselves in a similar situation. What makes the resort to direct controls in this case even more likely is that the main resource is likely to be labor, and it is very difficult for political and psychological reasons to *reduce* money wages where labor is not wanted under the emergency conditions. This leaves money wage increases as the indirect instrument for redeploying labor to where it is wanted; hence, the inflationary potential of such a policy. Wage controls and (at times) direct limitations of labor mobility may therefore be indicated.

Other Instruments

One of the most powerful instruments in the government's hands inheres in its roles as consumer, producer, and investor. In the United States, since the mid-fifties, all levels of government have been purchasing about one-fifth of the gross national product [10] and have been accounting for about the same proportion of gross fixed investment. In Western Europe, these proportions have been the same or higher—the government's share in investment being sometimes twice as high as here—while government-owned enterprises in the production sector are much more important than here. All this gives government considerable leverage in regard to promoting economic activity, stimulating depressed or backward areas (such as the South in Italy), influencing wage and labor standards, and so forth.

We have already had occasion to mention government's regulation of monopolistic industries and promotion (sometimes, restriction) of competition. This has been the American approach to monopoly: Regulate it if it is a "natural" one; otherwise, don't permit it to develop except in a number of specifically sanctioned exceptions. The European approach has been nationalization of the natural monopolies and of other concentrated industries and a more tolerant attitude toward private monopolies and cartels. In the final analysis, there is probably not much to choose between regulation of nominally private "public utilities" and their nationalized operation (see next section). As for anti-trust policies in the United States, their purposes and effects have been debated vigorously. Some feel that the policy's effects have been economically beneficial not only through its direct impact on some industries but also by way of example and deterrent for others. Others are more skeptical. Others feel that the chief benefits have been political—preventing undue concentrations of private power.[11]

NATIONALIZATION
AND PUBLIC ENTERPRISE

In the United States, the climate of opinion has been generally hostile to government—at any level, and especially the federal—engaging in production. As a result, there is relatively little public enterprise in this country. Even such industries as the telegraph and telephone services, radio and television broadcasting, airlines, railroads, and central banking, which are nearly always or at least frequently state-owned in other advanced countries, are privately owned here—though in all the mentioned cases, subject to close regulation by public authorities. Nonetheless, quite a few of the activities that compete with or replace actual or potential private enterprise are publicly owned and operated in the United States, ranging from the Post Office, through federal arsenals, power- [12] and water-distribution projects, various in-

[10] This ratio has remained quite stable since the middle fifties, but within total government purchases of goods and services the share of state and local government has been rising and by 1964 has almost reached the federal outlay.

[11] Again the reader is referred to Richard Caves, *American Industry: Structure, Conduct, Performance* (Englewood Cliffs, N.J.: Prentice-Hall, 1964), this series; Joe S. Bain, *Industrial Organization* (New York: Wiley, 1959); and Edward S. Mason, *Economic Concentration and the Monopoly Problem* (New York: Atheneum, 1964).

[12] In 1962, of the total electric power production in the United States (including production by industrial plants) 21.3 per cent was generated by publicly owned installa-

stitutions in the fields of credit and insurance, to locally owned public housing and urban transportation.[13] Though rarely thought to be such, education is a major "industry" where public operation predominates. And a very important publicly owned resource is forest lands,[14] together with the associated mineral, water, and recreational resources.

We saw in Chapter 3 that nationalization of major industries, once a cornerstone of the socialist program, has been largely abandoned as a goal by the present-day democratic socialist parties of Europe. Here we pause briefly to discuss nationalization [15] and public ownership as control instruments and to take a glimpse at some of their problems.

Retreat from Nationalization

Nationalization has been traditionally advocated for two kinds of reasons: general and particular. In the socialists' view—by now greatly attenuated—the general reasons for extensive nationalization were to minimize private ownership of the means of production and thereby to reduce the alleged evils of capitalism, including economic instability, labor strife, and maldistribution of wealth, income, and power. In the meantime, however, the realization has been growing that, on one hand, the inflated power of the state is also an evil, and that, on the other hand, capitalism and capitalists can be made to behave in the social interest. Thus, it has been realized that nationalization as such contributes relatively little to economic stability and that instruments of macro-economic planning would have to be invoked in a market economy however much or little nationalized. (However, it is true that a large public enterprise sector helps the government to pursue a contracyclical or a growth-generating investment policy.) As for redistribution, here too, the various tax and welfare instruments can accomplish much more than nationalization. As for power, it has come to be appreciated that in an industrial society a great deal of power resides with managers and labor leaders, regardless of who the nominal owner(s) of the firms might be. Nor, it has been discovered, is labor strife eliminated by nationalization. It is quite possible for conflicts to arise between a socialist government and labor unions in nationalized industries, as the British Labor Party found out while in power between 1945 and 1951.

The particular reasons pertain to individual industries. They may be

---

tions, of which 12.2 per cent were federal, 4.4 per cent were municipal (in 800 systems), and 4.6 per cent belonged to states, cooperatives, and other non-private entities. U.S. Department of Commerce, Bureau of the Census, *Statistical Abstract of the United States* (Washington, D.C.: Government Printing Office, 1964), p. 529.

[13] A brief survey of public enterprise in the U.S. may be found in Merle Fainsod, Lincoln Gordon, and Joseph C. Palamountain, Jr., *Government and the American Economy*, 3rd ed. (New York: Norton, 1959), pp. 737-751. See also Clair Wilcox, *Public Policies Towards Business* (Homewood, Ill.: Irwin, 1960).

[14] As of 1953, the federal government owned 22 per cent and state and local governments owned 5.6 per cent, of commercial forest land. *Statistical Abstract of the United States*, 1964, p. 681.

[15] Strictly speaking, nationalization is to be distinguished from *socialization*, the latter referring to ownership (or take-over) by any public authority, the former, to the national (federal) government. *Municipalization*, a form of socialization, and ownership by other levels of government below the national are frequently preferred over nationalization by advocates of public ownership as a way of avoiding undue concentration of power.

nationalized because they are unprofitable and inefficient and have little prospect of improving under private ownership. Such was the case, for example, with the British coal industry and railroads when they were nationalized by the Labor government immediately after World War II. By consolidating operations and pouring in large funds for re-equipment and research, the state can bring about improvement that was beyond the means of former owners. Alternatively, nationalization may be advocated not because the industry is sick but because, on the contrary, it is too strong and healthy for the public good—i.e., that it is a successful monopoly or exercises potential control over a vital area of the economy. It is for reasons such as these that electric power, transport, steel, munitions, and other industries are frequently nationalized. (In the U.S., the processing of fissionable materials is restricted to federally owned installations in order to maintain public control over this strategically important activity, though these may be operated by private firms under contract.) In such cases, an alternative to nationalization is government regulation, which is the preferred solution in the United States. It is difficult to say which is generally the better arrangement from the public's standpoint. More correctly, nationalization may not do away with the need for regulation, since those in control over state-owned industry still have to be made amenable to the general interest and accountable to political authority. These last problems are among the thorniest relating to public enterprise.[16]

The legal form that is widely regarded as most suitable for public enterprise is the *public corporation,* an autonomous entity, accountable to a ministry of the government and through the ministry to the legislature for general policy but not for detailed activity. Many examples are to be found in Western Europe, especially in the United Kingdom. In this country, on the federal level, the autonomous public corporation is less common; the Tennessee Valley Authority was one when first established in 1933 but later lost some of its autonomy.[17] The public corporation combines flexibility and at least the possibility of initiative with ultimate responsibility to the public. The best known public enterprise in the United States, the Post Office, is decidedly not a case in point, as it has virtually no autonomy and suffers from a great deal of interference from Congress and the Executive. If it is not the paragon of efficiency, it is also not a fair test of public enterprise, though often regarded as just that.[18]

[16] Three other very important reasons for nationalization must be mentioned. First, the government may assume ownership or control of private firms as a way of rescuing them in a severe depression. Thus, a large part of Italian nationalized enterprises came into the hands of the state in the thirties in this fashion. Second, nationalization may be primarily political—e.g., to take over, with or without compensation, the property of foreign nationals, especially of citizens of unfriendly countries. Such for instance, was the case with extensive nationalization in Egypt and Cuba in the early sixties. Third, the state may retain the monopoly of certain economic activities for fiscal purposes; e.g., state ownership of tobacco, salt, and match industries in some European countries.

[17] Cf. Fainsod *et al., op. cit.,* pp. 759ff.

[18] On the public corporation see *ibid.,* Chapter 24. A voluminous inquiry into the public corporation and other aspects of nationalization in Great Britain is William A. Robson, *Nationalized Industry and Public Ownership* (London: Allen & Unwin, 1960).

PLANNING AND CONTROL
IN SEVERAL COUNTRIES [19]

The positive concern of the federal government with the promotion of economic activity is as old as the Republic. Alexander Hamilton's *Report on the Subject of Manufactures* (1791) has remained a classic argument for the promotion of industry with the aid of such indirect instruments as tariffs and subsidies. And from George Washington's first administration until 1934, with the exception of some thirty years immediately before the Civil War, the protective tariff was a major instrument of American "planning" for industrialization. Another important tool for the pursuit of positive economic policy by the federal government was, for a long time, the vast amount of public land in its possession. The land was used successfully to encourage family farming (e.g., Homestead Act of 1862), to stimulate the construction of railroads, and even to induce states to set up schools of higher learning (Land Grant College Act of 1862).[20] The Great Depression turned attention to stabilization,[21] and after World War II Congress passed the Employment Act of 1946, which for the first time explicitly recognized the federal government's responsibility for the country's economic well-being. The government was charged with using "all practicable means . . . to foster and promote free competitive enterprise and the general welfare . . . and to promote maximum employment, production, and purchasing power."

The act created a *Council of Economic Advisers* to the President which analyzes economic trends and prospects and advises him on policy.[22] The strategy that all administrations—of both parties—have since followed, though in different degree, has been that of macro-economic planning of the "liberal" variety [23] and of promoting specific programs. The pursuit of both positive guidance and stabilization of the economy, and especially the bolder use of budget deficits to stimulate higher levels of business activity and employment and faster growth, has been more vigorous under the Kennedy and Johnson administrations. While one cannot speak of national planning in the United

---

[19] A convenient summary account will be found in L. A. Skeoch and David C. Smith, *Economic Planning: The Relevance of the West European Experience for Canada* (Montreal: Private Planning Association of Canada, 1963). Because of the great similarity in structure and institutions between the two economies, the authors' comments and conclusions regarding lessons for Canada usually also are relevant for the United States.

[20] A useful historical sketch of the promotion of business by the federal government will be found in Fainsod *et al., op. cit.,* Chapter 5.

[21] This is not to say that the objective of stabilization did not prompt important federal measures even before the thirties. Thus, the establishment of the Federal Reserve System in 1913 was a consequence of the serious financial panic of 1907.

[22] At the beginning of each year, in pursuance of the Employment Act, the President submits an *Economic Report* to the Congress. This *Report,* together with a much more detailed report to the President from the Council and with a substantial statistical appendix, is published early in the year and constitutes a valuable source of information on the state of the economy and on the administration's policies.

[23] I.e., paying respect to economic freedoms.

States in a more rigorous and comprehensive sense or with regard to the longer term—and it is not obvious that there is need for such planning, either —the federal government is deeply committed to "liberal planning" for stabilization and promotion of the general welfare, and is likely to remain so under any administration in the foreseeable future.

The Netherlands

Both the Netherlands and Sweden share with the United States democratic political structures, a preponderance of private enterprise, and an emphasis that the national government places on short-term stabilization as against long-term planning; but they differ considerably between themselves and from the United States regarding the methods and instruments of economic control. The case of the Netherlands is noteworthy because of the consistent use made of an elaborate econometric model for purposes of year-to-year stabilization planning.[24] The model consists of 36 equations and as many variables. The chief target variables are the surplus (deficit) of the balance of payments, employment, level of investment, the proportion of wages in the national income, and the price level. The main instrument variables are levels of direct and indirect taxes, government expenditures, the wage level, and credit. (Notice that these are all indirect controls available to other democratic governments—except for the wage level, a form of direct control which the Dutch authorities, unlike the United States government, have the power to set.)

The model was constructed by the Central Planning Bureau, an interdepartmental government agency. By means of the model, the Bureau prepares an annual set of projections indicating expected values of target variables on alternative assumptions with regard to values of the instrument variables, and submits it, first, to a Central Planning Commission, consisting of representatives of government departments and the public, and then to the Social and Economic Council. The latter, composed equally of representatives of employers, representatives of labor unions, and experts serving in their private capacities, is only an advisory body but in fact wields great power, including that of wage-setting. Its recommendation for the use of the various instruments then in fact constitutes the annual plan, though it has no legal force.[25]

Sweden

While Sweden has had a social democratic government since 1932, private enterprise is almost as prevalent in that country as in the United States. There is hardly any public enterprise other than the public utilities, although

[24]On econometric models for planning see *supra,* p. 58. We by-pass here long-term planning in the Netherlands; see Stanislaw H. Wellisz, "Economic Planning in the Netherlands, France, and Italy," *The Journal of Political Economy,* Vol. LXVIII, No. 3 (June 1960), pp. 252-256.

[25] More on Dutch short-term planning will be found in Wellisz, *loc. cit.,* pp. 263-268; Skeoch and Smith, *op. cit.,* Chapter 4; (Netherlands) Central Planning Bureau, *Central Economic Plan, 1961* (The Hague, August 1961); and books and articles by Jan Tinbergen, the chief architect of Dutch planning.

cooperatives are quite important in retail distribution and manufacturing (as well as other fields) in what is the classic country of cooperation. Welfare measures are also highly developed. Lately, Sweden has had the highest per capita national income in Europe.

Sweden has pioneered in the shaping of instruments for contracyclical policy and stabilization. A major step in this direction was the budget reform of 1937, which divided the government's budget into two parts—the current and capital budgets—in order to bring out the distinction between current consumption and investment by the state, and began the deliberate utilization of budgetary deficits and surpluses for stabilization purposes. Along with a number of more or less standard tools—general fiscal and monetary policy, public works, a standby emergency public works budget, loans for housing construction (90 per cent being financed by government credit), and extensive measures to promote labor mobility—Sweden has developed a distinctive instrument, the investment reserve. No mathematical model is used in this connection.

The key organization in the investment reserve system is the National Labor Market Board (NLMB)—like the Dutch Social and Economic Council, not a government bureau but a tripartite entity consisting of representatives of labor, employers, and government. The NLMB, together with 25 local Labor Market Boards and many regional offices, is responsible for the full employment program, collects information, prepares forecasts, stimulates labor mobility, and advises firms on location.

The investment reserve system is complex in detail but simple enough in principle. Firms receive tax incentives to set aside up to 40 per cent of their pre-tax profit in any year as an investment reserve. Of the amount so set aside, 46 per cent is deposited with the Central Bank and remains frozen there until officially released. The remaining 54 per cent is retained by the firm. When business conditions decline and increased investment activity becomes desirable, the Ministry of Finance decides how much of the investment reserves may be used and under what conditions and so informs the NLMB, which in turn gives permission to individual companies. The reserves must be used for approved types of investment projects, the two portions of the reserve being utilized in the same 46-54 ratio. Further incentives by way of accelerated depreciation write-offs and taxes are extended at this time in order to stimulate the actual use of the reserves for investment. Since 1963, the device has also been used to promote business in depressed areas regardless of general economic conditions.

The investment reserve system finds its rationale in the importance of internal funds for company financing and the instability of unregulated investment outlays over the business cycle. It is flexible regarding timing, amount released, and sector or region of impact. It works through the market and does not discourage efficiency.[26]

[26] A convenient account of Swedish stabilization policies and instruments is U.S. Congress, Joint Economic Committee, *Economic Policies and Practices:* Paper No. 5, *Unemployment Programs in Sweden* (Washington, D.C.: Government Printing Office, 1964). There also has been some long-range planning in Sweden, but only in very broad and general terms. The investment reserve device is also utilized in Finland, and something similar exists in the socialist market economy of Yugoslavia (Chapter 7). It has attracted the attention of economists in many advanced countries.

If the Netherlands and Sweden have stressed short-run stabilization that in either case perhaps only barely qualifies as "planning," France has developed in the postwar period and continues to practice the most elaborate and detailed planning system among the advanced Western countries, one that emphasizes the longer term and is more oriented toward growth than stabilization. The central institution in French planning is the General Commissariat (i.e., Commission) for Planning (G.C.P.), but many other bodies, governmental and multipartite, are also involved. As in Sweden, but in contrast to the Netherlands, no formal econometric model is employed.

Established as early as 1946 in order to plan the postwar reconstruction of the French economy, the G.C.P. soon became concerned with planning for the utilization of the European Recovery Program ("Marshall Plan") funds supplied by the United States. Four four-year plans have been so far drawn up and put into effect: 1947-1950 (extended to the end of the Marshall Plan in 1953), 1954-1957, 1958-1961, and 1962-1965. The fifth plan, to run this time for five years (1966-1970), is currently being drafted.

Two phrases frequently used in connection with French planning by its partisans are *économie concertée,* which may be translated as "a pre-concerted economy," and "indicative planning." The former denotes that the plan emerges as a broad consensus among various major groups in the society, while the term "indicative" is meant to stress that the planning provides only the framework and guidelines for future economic activity and does not attempt to force or coerce anyone to comply (as is the case with Soviet-style planning, which is accordingly termed "imperative"). Indicative planning, however, does not preclude the use of rather strong instruments by the government to carry out the plan, as we shall see.

The fundamental purposes of the plan are (1) to stimulate over-all economic growth, (2) to promote the modernization of the economy, and (3) to shape the sectoral, industrial, and regional pattern of production in more desirable directions, while (4) preserving full employment, stability, and balance of payments equilibrium. The Fourth Plan (1962-1965) also aimed to steer consumption somewhat in the "Galbraithian" direction—i.e., more in favor of public goods (education, public health, urban improvement) as against personal consumption. Short-term stabilization has been left to macroeconomic policy operating somewhat apart from the plan. (However, because of the augmented inflationary pressure, the Fifth Plan (1966-1970) aims to establish "indicative" targets for wages, prices and profits, thus taking the French planning process into a new and politically difficult direction.) The plan seeks to achieve the fundamental objectives in essentially two ways. (1) Its targets are supposed to be a set of consensus-based and mutually consistent prognoses, which, if taken seriously by all concerned, tend to reduce uncertainty about the future and to be self-fulfilling. (2) At the same time, the plan's targets are to be attained by the deliberate and purposeful use of a series of economic instruments at the government's disposal.

Drawing up the plan is a complex process which intentionally seeks to involve a large number of interested parties and professional experts. The process begins with the G.C.P. and the Economic and Financial Research Service of the Ministry of Finance preparing studies of the current situation and of medium-term and longer-term possibilities. Several alternative sketches of the plan are produced for consideration by the Investment and Planning Section of the Economic and Social Council, a multipartite body, and then by the executive branch of the government. After the government has laid down the directives for the plan, stipulated its main purposes and goals,[27] and has drawn up a balanced account for the plan's target year, the so-called Modernization Committees take over. These committees, about two dozen in number and multipartite in structure, concern themselves with individual sectors, industries, or problem areas. Their proposals are coordinated by the G.C.P. until a consistent plan emerges, leading eventually to approval by the government, consultation with the High Planning Council (also multipartite) and the Economic and Social Council, and final approval *in toto* by Parliament. The operative document that finally emerges in this fashion consists primarily of a series of growth targets for the economy as a whole, its main sectors by use of product (consumption, investment, etc.), and the various production sectors and industries. No production targets for individual firms are given (except for some of the larger nationalized public utilities), for doing so would transform the plan from an "indicative" to an "imperative" one.

It is clear even from this summary sketch that great emphasis is placed on consensus among government representatives, experts, and spokesmen for various interest groups. This in itself is an important instrument of plan execution in that it tends to maximize the acceptance of the plan's objectives by the public and to give the targets greater credibility. And in fact, for a country as politically diverse as France, the degree of consensus achieved around the plan has been notable, though there is no assurance that it will continue indefinitely.[28]

But in addition, the authorities dispose of an impressive arsenal of tools for executing the plan. First, some 35-40 per cent of all gross fixed investment involves either the "general government" sector or public enterprises, and together with the private investment financed by the state, the government has direct leverage over more than half of all investment in the country. Beyond this, the government has control over the larger loans and over stock issues and uses this power to ensure that priority in financing is given to economic activity conforming to the plan and its sectoral divisions. Tax exemptions of various kinds, depreciation write-off privileges, loan guarantees, and even subsidies are employed to the same end. Lastly, the government retains price controls over a number of key commodities and uses this power to increase compliance with the plan.

[27] Beginning with the Fifth Plan, the government must by law seek from Parliament approval of the plan's main objectives before addressing its Directives to the G.C.P.

[28] Hitherto, organized labor, which in France is in large part dominated by the Communist party, has been underrepresented in the various councils and committees. Were it more fully represented, consensus might be more difficult to reach. Also, French employer groups are beginning to show a less cooperative attitude towards the philosophy of planning.

The effectiveness of French planning has been intensely debated. Proponents point to the very high rate of growth of the French economy in the postwar period—one of the highest in Western Europe—as proof of success, recalling that in the interwar period the French economy was notoriously stagnant. Skeptics reply that Western European countries with no national planning at all, especially West Germany and Italy, have experienced even higher rates of growth during the postwar period. They also point out that the attainment of sectoral goals under the plans has not been uniformly close. And they express the fear that the consensus-producing machinery may have the harmful side effect of reducing competition. From the left there is also the criticism that the plan tends to aid the entrenchment of existing economic power and does nothing to redistribute income and wealth.[29]

Is the French planning experience exportable? In view of France's relatively high growth and virtual absence of unemployment during the fifties and early sixties, this question has been increasingly asked in such countries as the United States and Canada, which have had substantial unemployment and much lower growth rates, and the United Kingdom and Belgium, also with relatively low growth though without significant unemployment.

So far as the United States is concerned, the case for borrowing French planning methods is not at all obvious, even if we grant for the moment (which is in fact questioned, as we just saw) that national planning has made a considerable contribution to the very good performance of the French economy in the postwar years.

First, it is not clear that much is to be gained in the United States by setting a precise target for over-all economic growth some 4-5 years in advance. The duration of a presidential administration in this country is only four years; besides, any such definite commitment would be politically unwise if taken seriously by the public, and ineffectual, if not. To instill confidence and encourage capital formation, it is probably quite sufficient for the administration to convince the public that it will resolutely pursue measures within its powers to attain and maintain high employment, keep prices relatively stable, and stimulate growth. And while growth targets for specific industries and sectors may reduce some uncertainty regarding the future, they would not seem to be so desirable as to be set up in the face of very likely opposition of business and at the risk of the targets' being discredited through uneven attainment.

Equally important is the fact that some of the most important enforcement instruments are not available—or not to the same degree—to the federal government. Public investment at *all* levels of government accounts in this country for about one fifth of total fixed investment, or about half its relative

[29] French planning has already produced a substantial body of writing in English, let alone in French. John Hackett and Anne-Marie Hackett, *Economic Planning in France* (London: Allen & Unwin, 1963), is a thorough treatise. A brief critical analysis will be found in Wellisz, *loc. cit.*, pp. 268-273. A useful brief survey and analysis is P.E.P. (Political and Economic Planning), "Economic Planning in France," *Planning,* Vol. XXVII, No. 454 (August, 1961), p. 14, and also in Carl Landauer's textbook, *Contemporary Economic Systems* (Philadelphia: Lippincott, 1964), pp. 271-289.

importance in France, and attempts by an administration to establish tight control over it all would run counter to our federal political structure. Nor does the U.S. government exercise direct control over important prices in peacetime. Perhaps most significant, the very rigorous control over credit and stock issues that is exercised by the French government would hardly be voted by Congress or accepted by the financial and business communities in this country in normal times. Finally, attempts to reach consensus within industries on the French manner would tend to clash with our tradition of keeping business as competitive as possible wherever feasible.

SUMMARY

In its broadest meaning, public planning is the purposeful, deliberate, systematic shaping of economic phenomena by some public authority. It should not be confused with socialism or with nationalization; it exists in market economies as well as in command economies; some forms of it are quite compatible with economic freedoms and political democracy. Macro-economic planning aims at maintaining such conditions as full employment, price stability, and a desirable growth rate. Micro-economic planning deals with individual sectors, regions, and industries. The instruments of control or planning in a market economy include, among others, indirect controls (which work through the market mechanism) and direct controls (which attempt to thwart its operation) to achieve certain social goals. In the United States, national economic policy (not usually called "planning") works primarily through macro-economic planning, indirect controls, and specific programs. The Netherlands and Sweden have developed elaborate methods and institutions of short-term stabilization. France is the outstanding example of an advanced western country resorting to longer-term planning to control the direction and pace of its economic growth, using some distinctive procedures and instruments.

The Command Economy:

The USSR

The First World War gave Lenin his chance. Capitalizing on the country's war-weariness and the peasants' hunger for land, he and his Bolshevik (later, Communist) party seized power in Russia in November [1] 1917 and retained it through a prolonged, bloody civil war. Their ultimate aim was to re-do not only Russia but the whole world in the image of Marxian socialism and full communism—a world without want, classes, exploitation, injustice, and war. But first there were two paradoxes to be resolved. The Communists were a tiny minority in the population, some four-fifths of which consisted of backward and poor peasants who did not share communist values or goals. Thus, dictatorship and at least some coercion were unavoidable internally if the Communists were to remain in power and to pursue their own goals resolutely, which they fully intended to do. Second, the outside world, especially the advanced countries, did not oblige by following revolutionary suit, as the Communists had expected. Instead, the Soviet Union found itself isolated in an ideologically unfriendly world, angry at the expropriation of the large amount of foreign capital within Russia, and resentful of Moscow's unceasing attempts to export its revolution. These two facts—continuous struggle with an uncooperative population, particularly peasantry, at home and an

---

[1] It was still October by the Julian calendar then in effect in Russia; hence the name "October Revolution." The Tsarist regime had been overthrown the previous March ("February Revolution"); in the meantime, the country was ruled by a democratic "Provisional Government."

antagonistic relationship with most of the outside world—have profoundly affected Soviet economics as well as politics ever since.[2]

The Soviet economy at the time of the communist take-over presented a mixed picture. On one hand, it was predominantly agricultural, backward, and very poor on a per capita basis. On the other hand, thanks to very rapid industrialization since the 1880's and its large population, by 1917 Russia already had the fifth biggest industrial complex in the world, a relatively large heavy industry, and an appreciable nucleus of scientists and engineers. On the basis of this modern sector, and with the aid of millions of laborers to be drawn from the villages, rapid industrialization was to resume under the Soviets, according to the plans that were being drawn up and hotly debated[3] during the twenties. When Stalin took power at the end of that decade, he was determined to build up as quickly as possible the country's industrial and military might to ensure security from external attack and "the victory of socialism" within the USSR. To do so he proceeded in three main directions: (1) He put extreme pressure on the country, and especially on the peasants, to mobilize all resources and to devote as large a share of them as possible to capital formation (and, later, defense), almost heedless of the consumers' well-being. (2) He launched a series of Five-Year Plans—the first in 1928— and replaced the market economy and whatever then still remained of private enterprise (mostly in agriculture and small-scale production elsewhere) with a highly centralized command economy and almost complete state ownership of means of production. (3) He soon began a ruthless police terror which was to send millions into concentration camps and untold numbers to death. Whatever its real reasons, the terror served to enforce the public's often severe privations, the constraints on personal economic freedom, and the high degree of centralization of the economy.

Ever since then, the Soviet economy has always been in a hurry to raise itself—with relatively little outside help—from a position of comparative backwardness to one of pre-eminent industrial and military power. The Soviet leaders' ideology, though couched in Marxist and revolutionary terms, has been one of the prime instances of an industrializing ideology in modern times.[4] The haste with which Soviet industrialization has been conducted goes far to explain many of the characteristic features of the Soviet economy, such as the very high share of investment in the national product (high "investment rate") and the highest priority accorded to the development of the "heavy" industries. It also helps explain the rapid growth, the ambitiousness of the national plans, the constant pressure on the country's resources, and the chronic shortages of materials, equipment, and skilled labor. These in turn help explain the extreme centralization of the organizational structure in the form

[2] For much fuller descriptions and analyses of the Soviet economy the reader is referred to Abram Bergson, *The Economics of Soviet Planning* (New Haven: Yale University Press paperback, 1964); Robert W. Campbell, *Soviet Economic Power* (Cambridge: Houghton Mifflin, 2nd edition, 1966); and Alec Nove, *The Soviet Economy—An Introduction* (New York: Praeger, revised edition, 1965). The author thanks Professor Herbert S. Levine for valuable comments on this chapter.

[3] On these debates, see Nicolas Spulber, *Soviet Strategy for Economic Growth* (Bloomington: Indiana University Press, 1964) and Alexander Erlich, *The Soviet Industrialization Debate, 1924-1928* (Cambridge: Harvard University Press, 1960).

[4] On industrializing ideologies, see pp. 24-25.

of the command economy, although the authoritarian nature of the political faith and the ideological bias against the market mechanism doubtless also played a role in this regard. Finally, these consequences of haste help explain many of the Soviet economy's inefficiencies.

ORGANIZATION
OF THE SOVIET ECONOMY

Ownership

The Soviet economy is officially designated as "socialist" because of the predominance of public ownership of production assets. Notice that it is never referred to by Soviet spokesmen as "communist"—the term is reserved exclusively for the Marxist ultimate society of the future [5] which the USSR is now said to be in the process of "constructing."

The direct employment of one person by another is not permitted, except for domestic servants. Households own their personal possessions; they may also own deposits in savings banks, state bonds, and insurance policies. But all natural resources, including all land, are owned by the state, as is the bulk of reproducible capital goods. Yet in three sectors—agriculture, retail trade, and housing—there is also substantial non-state ownership, including private ownership. The situation in agriculture shall be taken up presently. As for retail trade, in 1964, state-owned stores accounted for 68 per cent of the value of retail sales, cooperative stores (under close government control, mostly rural), 28 per cent, and the *kolkhoz market,* 4 per cent. The last consists of a series of "farmers' markets," mostly in cities, to which peasants and collective farms may sell their own produce freely at unregulated prices. In housing, at the end of 1964, 64 per cent of all *urban* dwelling space was state-owned and (to a small degree) cooperative; the rest was privately owned for supposedly personal use. Most rural housing is privately owned.

A few other, and mostly quite minor, instances of private economic activity may be mentioned. Professionals—doctors, dentists, lawyers, teachers—are permitted to engage in private practice and often do. More numerous are various artisans and craftsmen working on their own account: tailors and seamstresses, cobblers, carpenters, and the like. There is a great deal of "moonlighting" by state employees. Last but not least, there seems to be a large amount of illegal trading and even manufacturing for private profit. The extremely severe penalties, up to death, meted out for "economic crimes"—such as embezzling and pilfering from the state, bribe-taking and bribe-giving—suggest that Soviet man is no less self-serving and no more civic-minded than Western man despite decades of education in socialist morality.

[5] For the Marxist distinction between "socialism" and "communism," see pp. 32-33.

The whole Soviet economy—with the exception of the household sector —can be depicted as an enormous bureaucratic pyramid, or a series of pyramids with a common apex. All the significant decisions are made at the top. Indeed, all of the most important ones and a surprising number of detailed ones are made by the dictator himself, as was the case under Stalin and Khrushchev, or by a very few men in the brief periods (such as the present) when there seems to have been no single boss. These men are (or were) at once leaders of the Communist party of the Soviet Union and of the Soviet government. This is one of the senses in which the party rules the country. The bottom tier of this pyramid consists of hundreds of thousands of individual firms (including farms) whose main task is to carry out directives from above. Between the bottom tier and the top of the pyramid there is a welter of planning, administrative, financial, statistical, and other bureaucratic hierarchies, not the least important of which is that of the Communist party itself and closely related organizations.

The most important planning agency of the Soviet government is the State Planning Commission of the USSR, usually known by its Russian abbreviation *Gosplan USSR*. The "USSR" in the title indicates that this is the commission on the national level; there is a Gosplan for each of the constituent republics,[6] as well as province and district planning offices. Gosplan USSR prepares both the long-term and the short-term plans [7] and in fact decides many other issues of economic policy, although in theory it is only an advisory body within the government. A most powerful institution, it does not, however, have complete monopoly of planning even at the highest level. Other high-level bodies concern themselves with planning construction (a very important sector in a rapidly growing economy) and many other specialized areas and activities, such as research and development. The State Commission for the Supply of Materials and Equipment is in charge of distributing those materials and equipment that are centrally allocated; but since almost every important producer good is centrally allocated—there are some 20,000 such commodities—this is a very powerful organization indeed. Like Gosplan, the other planning agencies usually constitute large hierarchical organizations on a territorial basis. Still other planning bodies concern themselves with the problems of individual republics or large regions, cutting across sectors, industries, and functional areas.

[6] The Union of Soviet Socialist Republics (USSR) is legally a federation of fifteen republics, which are in fact much less autonomous than the American states, however. By far the largest and most important of them is the Russian Socialist Federated Soviet Republic (RSFSR), which accounts for over three-fourths of the area and some 55 per cent of the population of the USSR. The second most populous, the Ukrainian Soviet Socialist Republic, has 20 per cent of the USSR's population, while the least populous (and economically one of the most advanced), the Estonian SSR, has only one half of one per cent. Readers interested in the political structure and processes of the Soviet Union are referred to Merle Fainsod's very thorough *How Russia Is Ruled* (Cambridge: Harvard University Press, revised edition, 1963) or the concise account in Gwendolyn M. Carter, *The Government of the Soviet Union* (New York: Harcourt, Brace & World, 1962).

[7] This statement as well as all others describing the organizational structure of the Soviet economy, except as otherwise indicated, refers to the situation following the reorganization of October 1965.

But the planning and day-to-day management of individual sectors or industries of the economy is done by so-called ministries, of which there are several dozen.[8] Each ministry is in charge of a hierarchical organization, at the bottom tier of which are the individual enterprises. There are many other government departments with authority in economic affairs, but they must remain unmentioned here for lack of space. If by now you are beginning to suspect that there is a great deal of jurisdictional overlap and friction within the over-all organizational pyramid, and that confusion (enhanced by frequent re-organizations) is as much the rule as order, you are beginning to grasp the nature of Soviet economic organization.

Within the pyramid there is relatively little communication horizontally, even among firms, but there is a large flow of messages vertically. The upward-flowing messages carry, in great volume and detail, data about the state of the economy, and particularly about the execution of past directives, and requests for permission to act—information that is essential for the top authorities on which to base plans and other decisions. The equally detailed information flowing downward consist of specific directives, instructions, and permissions (or denials thereof). Communication lines tend to be long, causing delays in adjustment to changing conditions. The *Central Statistical Administration USSR* and its many regional and local offices collect an enormous number of periodic and occasional reports, process them, and channel the data upward to the many planning, financial, and administrative authorities. It—and the *USSR Ministry of Finance*—set reporting and statistical standards for all economic units.

The Industrial Firm

In industry, the basic production unit—called the "enterprise" in Soviet usage even though it has relatively little scope to be enterprising—usually consists of a single factory.[9] The manager ("director") of a Soviet enterprise does not have to contend with any independent labor union and therefore has great authority with regard to the workforce as compared with his Western counterpart. But in most other matters the Soviet manager and the enterprise as such have relatively little freedom of action.

The chief task of the enterprise is to carry out directives from above. These directives, usually formalized as the enterprise's plan for the year (or quarter, or month), pertain primarily to output, inputs, finances, and investment, and *in toto* govern the firm's activities in great detail. (In September 1965, the Soviet regime announced certain reforms, to be put into effect over the ensuing several years, which are eventually to grant somewhat greater autonomy to industrial enterprises. We shall return to discuss them briefly on

[8] This is so since October 1965, and was so before July 1957. From 1957 to 1965, industrial enterprises were mostly subordinated to regional authorities (sovnarkhozes), of which there were at first just over 100 and later somewhat under 50.

[9] In recent years there has been a tendency to combine several—usually smallish—plants into larger enterprises in order to benefit from some efficiencies of larger-scale management. The amalgamated enterprises are usually referred to as "firms" or "associations."

p. 96. How and to what extent the reforms will be carried out remains to be seen. The present section relates the situation as it has been up to now.)

The industrial enterprises' plan usually includes two kinds of directive with regard to output: (1) a global target ("gross value of output") expressed in supposedly constant prices, by which the enterprise's over-all performance has been primarily measured; and (2) production targets for individual commodities, usually expressed in physical terms, whose number varies with the character of the commodities produced and is often quite large. Management is strongly induced by means of monetary bonuses and other rewards and pressured in other ways to meet and to exceed these output targets—in Soviet parlance, "to fulfill and overfulfill the production plan"—and it tends to respond, often at the expense of other desiderata, such as cost or quality. Notice also that the output targets refer to production, not sales; thus, whether anyone has any use for its products may be of little concern to a given enterprise.

With regard to inputs, the enterprise is typically assigned a maximum limit for the number of persons it may employ and for the amount it may spend on wages per month. It is allowed to consume no more than certain amounts of individual important materials and fuel per unit of output. But as we have already mentioned, most important materials and fuel are allocated (rationed) to the enterprise in predetermined quantities, anyway.

Soviet enterprises use money and pay or receive prices and wages (see below). Since the prices (wages) of all inputs and outputs are fixed and known at the time that the directives (plans) are drawn up, it is a relatively simple matter also to establish targets for unit cost of production and for aggregate profits (or losses). Most of the planned profits go to the state; but the enterprise is encouraged to make "above-plan" profits, a considerable part of which may be retained by the enterprise. If the profits earned and retained according to plan are not sufficient to pay for the planned investment in fixed or working capital during the period, the state grants additional money for the purpose. Notice that up to now the enterprise has not been paying any interest to the state on the state's investment in it, nor has it had to repay the principal sum of such investment.[10]

The plans (directives) cannot possibly cover every detail of the enterprise's operation, so it is necessary to provide guidance to management for whatever decisions it may have to take on its own. Collectively known by the Russian abbreviation *khozraschet,* these rules enjoin the enterprise to manage its own finances, to keep books, to be solvent (unless otherwise instructed by its superiors), and to maximize its profits or minimize its losses within its very limited range of choice. But "the plan" always comes first, and the enterprise's range of choice pertains to little more than control over obvious waste. It is in this very narrow sense that one must understand the Soviet notion— at least as held hitherto—of profits (losses) as a "synthetic indicator" of managerial efficiency.

Agriculture

More complex is the organizational structure in agriculture. The state farm (*sovkhoz*) is organized and run somewhat like an industrial firm in that it is state-owned, its labor force is hired for wages, and it is subject to rigid

10 On the enterprise's relations with banks, see p. 82.

production plans (although, of course, also more subject to the vagaries of the elements). In 1962, sovkhozes accounted for a third of total agricultural marketings, less of total agricultural production.

One half of all the agricultural marketings in 1962 were made by collective farms (sing. *kolkhoz*), a peculiarly Soviet and historically very important type of production unit. Nominally cooperatives whose members are individual peasant households of a village or several neighboring villages, the kolkhozes were in fact forced by Stalin on the peasants and have been since closely managed and controlled by the government. To understand their role in the Soviet economy and their problems, we must go back once again to the late twenties.

As Stalin prepared to begin the great industrialization drive, he realized that its success would depend on a sharp increase in the state's acquisition of farm products in order to feed the cities that were soon to grow rapidly and to provide increasing surpluses for export to buy machinery abroad. But there was no assurance that the peasants—then farming in traditional ways—would comply, especially since Stalin was not prepared to devote large resources to "bribe" them. So, at the end of 1929, he launched a feverish collectivization drive. In the course of a few years virtually all of the country's peasants were forced, mostly against their will and sometimes with considerable violence, to join collective farms, surrendering their livestock and other major assets in the process. In the long run, these large farms were intended to become highly mechanized and efficient producers. But from the very beginning their main function was to deliver produce (chiefly, grain) to the state at minimal cost to the latter, thereby providing a large part of the economic resources for industrialization. At the same time, he compelled the peasants to work for the kolkhozes, which they did reluctantly and carelessly because of the very low remuneration, faulty connection between effort and pay, and because they preferred to work their private plots (on which more presently).

The results were in part successful and in part disastrous. The state was indeed able to obtain greatly increased amounts of produce at very little direct cost to itself. But the collectivization drive precipitated an immediate drop in output and widespread slaughter of livestock by the peasants. At the same time there was a sharp initial decline in the peasants' consumption level, at time leading to famines in the countryside as the government relentlessly claimed and collected its share of produce. The stagnation of agricultural production and the peasants' economic misery continued until the end of Stalin's rule. Although for a while after Stalin's death, during the mid-fifties, his successors managed by dint of more favorable policies to raise agricultural production by about 50 per cent, soon a new and still too low plateau was reached. The low productivity of agriculture remains a serious problem of the Soviet economy.

The collective farm is a very large production unit, containing on the average some 15,000 acres of agricultural land, of which some 7,300 acres are sown to crops, and over 400 peasant households—as well as about 3,000 animals (excluding fowl) and numerous structures and machines. The kolkhozes are still required to make deliveries to the state at low prices, though not nearly so low as in Stalin's day. They are told when, and how, to sow, cultivate, and harvest. These and many other forms of incessant pressure and interference from the local authorities have been among the chief reasons for the kolkhozes' lack of incentive, drive, and efficiency.[11]

The peasants are still obligated to work for the kolkhozes and may not freely leave them. For their work they receive during the year points of sorts. When the results of the year's farming are known, and after the obligatory deliveries to the state have been made and the required addition to the farm's capital has been set aside, most of the remainder is distributed, in kind and in cash, among the peasants in proportion to their accumulated points. Only in the wealthier kolkhozes are the peasants paid in cash at guaranteed rates and without waiting for the end of the year.

There is yet another side to the kolkhozes however. Each peasant household is permitted to work a tiny plot (up to 1 acre), to raise what it wishes on it (though it is allowed to keep no draft animals and only one milk cow), and freely to dispose of the produce, including selling it on the "kolkhoz market." [12] Because they are relatively so profitable, these tiny plots attract much of the peasants' time and effort, often at the expense of his working for the kolkhoz. Non-peasants are also allowed small plots. Altogether, private plots occupy only 3 per cent of the total sown area but absorb some 40 per cent of agricultural work and account for about one third of total farm output. This remarkable feat is explained by (1) much higher productivity of land and animals (though not of labor) on the private plots thanks to the greater care lavished on them, and (2) the fact that the private plots concentrate on higher value products, especially meat, milk, and eggs, obtaining the feed in large measure from outside the plots.

The Party

The top party leaders are also the highest government officials. The provincial and district party secretaries are the local bosses, though they are watched closely by *their* party superiors. There is a party cell in every enterprise or institution of any size. Thus, while party members comprise only 5 per cent of the population, they include within their ranks the vast majority of the important and the influential. The ambitious join the party for the sake of advancement, for party members have preference in appointment to responsible posts.

In the economic domain, local party authorities pass on all important personnel appointments. Local party cells are expected to lead enterprises to ever higher successes, to ensure ideological purity and political reliability, and to maintain continuous watch for slackness and transgressions of all sorts. Regional party bosses act as economic trouble-shooters, coordinators, and arbiters in their domains, and as champions of "their" enterprises against outsiders.

[11] In March, 1965, measures were taken to raise farm prices and to reduce administrative pressure on kolkhozes in order to raise productivity and efficiency. Indeed, by 1965 even the prices paid for obligatory deliveries had been raised to rather high levels in relation to world prices and are low chiefly in relation to the very high production costs in the kolkhozes.

[12] See p. 75.

Important as it is, the party is only one agency of supervision, surveillance, and control in the Soviet Union. There are innumerable others—ranging from the secret police to the local bank—that inspect the enterprise's affairs for adherence to plan and compliance with the law.

The Household; Labor

The households, at once consumers and providers of labor services, are tied to the production sector via markets for consumer goods and labor. The state decides what consumer goods and in what quantities will be produced [13] and places them on sale, under normal conditions without rationing and at more or less equilibrium prices. The consumer can "take it or leave it" at the quoted prices, though he is naturally limited to what the authorities choose to make available in the official stores in the given locality. Thus, generally speaking, there is freedom of consumer choice even if not consumer sovereignty. Similarly, the individual in his capacity as worker can usually select and change his job, being guided by the wages or salaries offered in other jobs.[14] And accordingly, wages and salaries are so set by the planners in the long run as to help deploy labor among occupations, levels of skill, industries, and regions in conformance with the planners' intentions. In sum, there is freedom of household choice in a broad sense, though not household sovereignty.[15]

There are good reasons for freedom of household choice in the USSR (as elsewhere). It is simpler for the state and preferable for the household if consumer goods are distributed in orderly markets with the exercise of free consumer choice and with the aid of money rather than by means of rationing. And it is much more satisfactory for the individual if he is free to choose and change jobs by means of direct assignment of individuals to jobs. There have been, however, very important exceptions to the principle of household choice in Soviet history. Consumer goods were rationed from 1929 to 1935 and from 1941 to 1947. Urban housing, very scarce throughout most of the Soviet period, has been rationed throughout and continues to be. As for labor, we have already seen that peasants may not leave collective farms without official permission, and that many millions were sentenced to forced labor (especially between 1930 and 1956). Even "free" workers were, between 1940 and 1956, formally—though not necessarily de facto—frozen in their jobs.

Thus, the economics of the Soviet worker's household is essentially the same as that of one in any other system, keeping in mind that it may acquire virtually no capital goods (nor, of course, shares of stock). It may, however, save any portion of its income and may invest its savings in state-owned savings banks, in state-issued bonds, and in private or cooperative housing for its own occupancy.

Nearly all workers and employees belong to labor unions, but these

[13] Except the goods traded in the *kolkhoz* market.

[14] In fact, a major problem of the Soviet economy in the sixties, as in the thirties, is excessive labor turnover as workers move from job to job in search of better pay, working conditions, housing, and availability of consumer goods.

[15] For the meaning of these terms, see pp. 8-10.

are very different from what we know in the West. Not independent in any real sense, the Soviet labor unions are just another of the regime's many arms. Their main purpose is to spur labor productivity and to do their part in indoctrination and propaganda. Their influence on wages is minimal. The right to strike exists in name but not in fact. Yet, at the factory level the union local may perform an important function in supporting the grievances of individual workers against management.

Soviet workers and employees are eligible for paid vacations, sickness and maternity leaves, (relatively modest) old-age pensions, and other fringe benefits. Many college-level students receive scholarships, while tuition is free. Old-age pensions were extended to cover all collectivized peasants only in 1964. The whole population is eligible for free medical care and hospitalization. There is no unemployment insurance on the premise that there is no unemployment—though there is a fair amount of frictional unemployment, while many persons (chiefly housewives in smaller towns) stay out of the labor force because of lack of employment opportunities.

Money

The Soviet economy uses money very much like any other economy. In effect, there are two kinds of money, though of the same monetary unit: [16] *currency,* which circulates almost exclusively within the household sector and in transactions between households and the state, and *bank money,* which circulates almost exclusively within the state sector—i.e., between state enterprises and agencies. Of course, currency and bank money are constantly converted into each other—to allow enterprises to pay wages, or by way of depositing the receipts of retail stores in banks—but only under strict controls. The reason for this distinction between and careful segregation of two kinds of money is (1) to prevent the over-issue of currency which might lead to inflationary pressures in the household sector, and (2) to maintain strict control over the activity of enterprises and state agencies. Indeed, such control is a main function of the banking system, and especially of the USSR State Bank (*Gosbank*)—with its thousands of branches—which at once is the bank of currency issue and has a virtual monopoly on all commercial banking.

Prices

The *kolkhoz* market is the only significant sector in the Soviet economy where prices move freely in response to demand and supply. In all other instances prices, including wage rates, are officially fixed ("planned"). In the two markets in which the state deals with the household sector, and where there is substantial household choice, those for consumer goods and labor services, prices are roughly so set as to equate demand and supply for individual goods or types of labor, as we have seen. By contrast, the prices which the state pays to a *kolkhoz* for farm products are deliberately set below equilibrium levels, and the supply is sustained by imposing compulsory deliveries on the farms. The fiscal levy on the peasantry that the low farm

[16] The monetary unit is the ruble; it is divided into 100 kopeks. Since 1961, it has been equal to U.S. $1.11 according to the official (Soviet) exchange rate. The ruble is not freely convertible into gold or foreign exchange.

prices represent continues to be large, though not nearly so important a source of the state's financial resources that it was in Stalin's day.

Prices are used within the state sector itself as well. Their main purpose is to facilitate accounting and thereby to check on the activity of individual enterprises. The method of price-setting has been set and influenced by the Marxian labor theory value. Until 1965, returns to non-labor factors of production—rent on land and other natural resources, interest on capital—either have not been accounted for at all, or only nominally.[17] Thus, the whole cost of producer goods (or consumer goods before they enter the distribution stage) consists directly or indirectly (through the cost of materials) of wage cost. To arrive at the fixed price of a given producer good, the planners calculate its anticipated average cost of production for the country as a whole (or, for bulky goods, for a region) and add a profit margin to that figure. In 1963, this profit on the average added about 12.5 per cent to the cost of production of industrial goods and in the aggregate constituted about 30 per cent of the state's financial resources (exclusive of depreciation reserves). But not much effort is made to set *producer goods prices* at equilibrium levels, let alone to express the goods' relative scarcities from the standpoint of the economy. Consequently, although widely used for accounting at all levels, Soviet producer goods prices are poor guides to the efficient use of resources.

In the case of consumer goods produced in the state sector, their *retail* prices usually also contain an excise tax—known as the *turnover tax*—which at once serves to build up prices of individual goods to equilibrium levels (as mentioned) and constitutes the main form of revenue in the government's budget.[18]

SHORT-TERM PLANNING AND OPERATION

The purpose of Soviet short-term plans is primarily to coordinate the activities of the many thousands of economic units—i.e., to substitute for the market mechanism's short-term functions. In this it differs sharply from the medium- and long-term plans—five and more years in duration—whose object is to lay down the directions and time-rates of economic development.

One-Year Plans

The drawing-up of a one-year plan is an extremely laborious process that extends over nearly the whole of the preceding year and is not really completed

[17] On the changes announced in 1965 in this regard, see p. 96.

[18] About one-third of the price paid by the consumer in official stores is accounted for by the turnover tax. A few producer goods, especially petroleum and products, also carry a substantial turnover tax. In 1963, the turnover tax brought in 38.5 per cent of the government budget's revenue, the tax on profit, 28.7 per cent. One third of the state's profits were not paid into the budget; taking this into account, the turnover tax and profits were of almost equal importance as financial resources for the state.

until well into the plan year (if at all). But in essence the procedure and method are simple enough. To begin with, the regime's leaders indicate to the planners (and with advice from the latter) the main outlines of the economy for the coming year: the desired increase of the national product and of the outputs of the main sectors and industries; distribution of the national product between consumption, investment, defense, and other major uses; distribution of investment by main industries; average consumption level of households; locational trends; and, last, but not least, the production targets for a series of the most important commodities. These *political goals* for the coming year in part derive from the targets of the longer-term plan then in effect, and in part from the wishes and policies of the leaders at the given moment. Even the initial, political goals must have some economic basis. Thus, the indicated rate of growth must be attainable; the volume of investment must be adequate to bring it about; the share of the national product going into consumption must be consistent with the planned average consumption level; and so forth.

It is the planners' job to translate these political goals into precise, detailed, and consistent production targets and directives for thousands of individual commodities and hundreds of thousands of enterprises for the coming year. The result of their efforts is a hierarchy of one-year plans for individual enterprises, ministries, republics, and the national economy as a whole. The planners also draw up a parallel hierarchy of *supply plans* which determine the physical allocation of most important materials and items of equipment among potential users. Incidentally, one of the chief—and rarely fully solved —problems of Soviet planning is that of coordinating these two plans, as they clearly must be if the economy is to function smoothly. Our sketch will concentrate on the production plan, however.

In addition to the political goals for the year, the central planners have two other kinds of information that permit them to proceed with their work. First, they know, though not always accurately, the economy's resources and productive capacity for the year. Second, they have many thousands of input-output ratios—in Soviet parlance, *norms*—which state the quantities of certain materials, labor, and equipment required to produce a unit of a certain product. Some of the norms stem from past experience; others, from engineering calculations. Finally, what greatly facilitates their job of drawing up the plan is the fact that the *changes* in production from year to year are not likely to be great.

The actual procedure involves, among other things, the sending down of a draft or sketch of a plan to lower levels in the hierarchy and receiving counter-suggestions from below. This is accompanied by a great deal of bargaining vertically between adjoining levels, as subordinates aim to exact relatively "easy" plans for themselves, while pressure for the opposite is brought to bear from the top down. By far the most laborious task faced in formulating the one-year plan at all levels is that of achieving *internal consistency*— that is to say, ensuring that all requirements for individual factors or commodities are matched by anticipated availabilities (from current production, inventories, or imports)—the job that in the market economy is performed by the market mechanism. In performing this task, the planners do not refer to relative prices or profitabilities. Rather, they utilize in physical terms an essentially very simple form of account, the so-called *material balance,* which lists on one side all the anticipated availabilities of a given good and on the other, all the expected requirements. In turn, the requirements and availabilities of the given good are linked to those of other individual goods by means of the norms, so that all the material balances are supposedly mutually consistent. If the two sides of a given material balance match, all is fine. But they rarely do at first, and typically the sum of the requirements exceeds the sum of the availabilities.

The process of "balancing" the material balances takes up much time and effort, especially since the adjustment of one balance often calls for numerous adjustments in many others. For example, if the requirements for copper initially exceed its expected availability, the amounts of copper to be allotted to various copper users may be cut back. In this case, the relative priority ratings of the users from the standpoint of national importance are involved. Alternatively, more resources may be shifted into copper production, or additional goods may be earmarked for export in order to purchase more copper abroad. These and other likely adjustments will affect material balances for goods other than copper, which in turn will affect yet others (perhaps also copper again), and so on indefinitely.[19]

In practice, only a limited number of "rounds" of adjustments can be undertaken. Considering that in recent years the central planners and supply allocators have been operating with nearly 20,000 material balances, you can imagine the enormity of the job and the imperfect internal coordination of the final plan. Moreover, even if a reasonably *consistent* plan should be produced, there is nothing in the method to suggest that it will also be a statically or dynamically efficient one—i.e., that the available resources will be so deployed as to maximize the achievement of the plan's goals or obtain the most growth from resources devoted to growth. Eventually, at times considerably after the beginning of the plan year, the individual firm receives *its* plan, its set of targets and directives for the year.

Operating Problems

Whatever its appearance on paper, in practice this system of short-term planning and management operates very poorly in many respects. This is not only the conclusion of outside observers; it is also the opinion of many economists in the USSR and other East European countries, whose criticisms have been persistent and often extremely sharp. What are the main faults?

To begin with, the internal coordination of the plans, and between the production and the supply plans, is often quite imperfect. This leads to bottlenecks, much idle capacity, unwanted inventories, and other waste of resources. Not infrequently, firms are ordered to produce goods for which there is no demand. Yet because of the tight centralization of decisions and the com-

---

[19] Those familiar with input-output methods will recognize that the problem of adjustment can be solved mathematically with the aid of an "inverse matrix" of coefficients. However, in practice this would not be easy because of the great detail of Soviet planning and because it may be desirable to introduce judgment at some points.

plexity of the system, corrections can be made only very slowly and with much difficulty. And if made, they tend to disrupt the smooth working of the enterprises. Thus, a common complaint of directors is that their plans are constantly revised, which would be bad enough in any case, but is particularly unsettling under Soviet conditions where materials are very hard to obtain.

Second, since management's bonuses induce it to maximize physical output at the expense of other desiderata, cost tends to be overlooked and quality tends to be depressed. Also, the enterprise tends to produce that product mix which maximizes its output in planned units rather than that which is highest in demand by customers. For example, ordered to produce as many pairs of skis as possible, Soviet enterprises have been prone to produce too many children's skis and too few skis for adults. This is inconvenient enough for the consumer. But when the good is a producer good, its low quality and incorrect specifications can have an adverse chain effect on several subsequent stages of production.

These faults have been aggravated by two other factors. First, the firm's plan is to *produce,* not to sell, a certain quantity of the product(s); hence, the customer's demand counts for little. Second, there being a general shortage of goods, the firm usually has little difficulty in disposing of its products though they be of poor quality or are obsolete in design.

The emphasis on maximum current production has another damaging effect. It causes the enterprises to resist innovations that may disrupt the flow of output or endanger plan fulfillment. The firm has little to gain from an innovation because the positive results—say, profits—will be taken by the state, while the risk of losing bonuses if something goes wrong remains with the management. Even worse, the next plan will only raise the targets accordingly, thus depriving the enterprise of the innovation's benefits. If the Soviet economy has nevertheless been experiencing rapid technological progress, this fact is to be credited, first, to the building of many new plants where there is yet no management to resist innovation and, second, to continuous pressure on management from the top for modernization of production processes and products.

These defects have been with the Soviet economy since its inception, but only after the relaxation of political controls in the mid-fifties did there appear open and widespread proposals for the system's improvement. Toward the end of this chapter we shall discuss some of these proposals as well as the reforms that were announced in 1965.

ECONOMIC GROWTH

In its concentrated drive to attain technological leadership and industrial primacy in the world, the USSR has employed comprehensive medium- and long-term plans—tools in whose development the USSR pioneered decades before they became a standard feature of most countries' development program. True, the long-term ("general") plans—10-15-20 years in duration—have been little but gross projections and guidelines for development, and in most cases were quickly rendered obsolete by the course of events. The medium-term plans have been five-year plans (FYP's), except for one seven-year plan.[20]

Medium-term Planning

The FYP's have represented the formal expression of the major goals and priorities of the Soviet leadership, such as:

—very high over-all rates of growth in order to reduce and eventually eliminate the gap in per capita productivity between the Soviet Union and the advance capitalist countries, particularly the United States;

—high priority for industrial development, and within industry, to heavy industry, and within heavy industry, to those branches—such as fuel, steel, machine-building—which contribute most to further industrialization and military power;

—emphasis on rapid increase in military power, including of course nuclear weapons and rocketry;

—universal primary education and large-scale training in technical, scientific, and vocational skills, especially those that would further the just-mentioned goals;

—the attainment of economic self-sufficiency vis-à-vis the outside world, both for defensive and for ideological reasons (though this goal was perforce modified in regard to the other communist countries after World War II).

For a long time, consumption held a low priority in this scheme of things, while agriculture, as we have seen, was relied upon to supply resources for industrialization. This occasioned such a low standard of living for the population and such stagnation in agriculture that these two sectors and supporting branches of industry have had to be accorded considerably more attention since Stalin's death.

The core of the FYP is the investment plan, which specifies the volume of capital formation over the five years, its distribution by industries and regions, and many of the larger individual construction projects. Much attention is devoted to the lines of technical advance. But because of the faulty price structure and the lack of appropriate guidelines in Soviet economic theory, as well as many gross errors and much undue haste, this investment planning and the selection of production technologies has not been very efficient.[21]

The following differences between medium-term and short-term planning should be noted. (1) Over five (or seven) years there is considerably more opportunity to shuffle resources, let alone to expand total resources significantly, than over one year. Hence, the element of political choice of goals is much more important in regard to the medium-term plan. (2) The FYP needs to be drawn up in considerably less detail than the one-year plan; especially since (3) the targets of the FYP do not constitute directives to any producers in the economy—such directives are later elaborated in the one-year plans.

[20] First FYP—October 1928-1932, 2d FYP—1933-1937, 3d FYP—1938-1942 (cut short by war in 1941), 4th FYP—1946-1950, 5th FYP—1951-1955, 6th FYP—1956-1960 (abandoned by 1957), Seven-Year Plan—1959-1965; a FYP for 1966-1970 is to follow.

[21] Cf. Bergson, *op. cit.,* Chapter 11.

As important as the FYP's have been in Soviet history for staking out the main lines of economic development and for propelling growth, their record of fulfilling exact targets is quite uneven. Of the seven put into effect so far, none can be said to have reasonably closely attained all the important goals.[22] The blame lies with overly ambitious goals, poor planning, faulty execution, and—not the least—the turbulence of Soviet history since 1928.

The Record Since 1928

What, then, has been the record of Soviet growth since 1928, the year in which the economy had already fully recovered from the effects of the Civil War and the accompanying disastrous economic policies, and in which the first FYP officially began? The country is bigger now, having added about 2 per cent to its vast territory as well as 12 per cent to its population in the course of annexations between 1939 and 1945 (mostly in Eastern Europe). From 1928 to 1966, the Soviet Union's population increased by somewhat over one-half, from 150 million to 232 million (beginning-of-year figures). Actually, this increase over 38 years is much smaller than what one would expect from the annexations and the high rates of natural increase during most of the period. The explanation lies with two demographic disasters. Taking into account both an increase in deaths and births below the expected "normal" level, we find that the collectivization crisis of the early thirties set the Soviet population back by some 10 million, and the Second World War and its immediate aftermath, by 40-50 million. The latter figures, on the order of the population of France at the present time, is also an indication of the enormous damage inflicted by the war on the Soviet economy. But economic recovery was rapid; the war set Soviet economic growth back by perhaps as little as six years (and population growth by some fifteen years).[23]

The composition of the population has changed greatly. In 1928, it was some 80 per cent agricultural and rural; by 1966, it had become more urban than rural and more non-agricultural than agricultural. In absolute numbers, the urban population increased more than 4½ fold, from 27.6 million to about 125 million. The educational level of the population rose sharply.

Even apart from wartime and postwar reconstruction, the Soviet economy grew far from smoothly under the FYP's;[24] more irregular was the growth of individual sectors, especially those with lower priority (such as agriculture). But it is not always easy to tell just how fast the growth was. The official Soviet series for national income, industrial production, and other "aggregates" are more often than not unreliable, sometimes very greatly exaggerating the actual growth, insofar as Western observers have been able to determine. The recomputations of aggregative series for the Soviet economy that various Western economists have consequently undertaken have given us a fairly clear picture of its growth, except that these estimates are sometimes

[22] For a convenient synoptic survey of goal attainment under the FYP's see Bergson, *op. cit.*, Table 5.2, p. 84, and Naum Jasny, *Essays on the Soviet Economy* (New York: Praeger, 1962), Table 6, p. 266.

[23] See G. Grossman, "Thirty Years of Soviet Industrialization," *Soviet Survey* (October-December, 1958), discussion of "effective years," p. 16.

[24] Cf. Naum Jasny, *Soviet Industrialization, 1928-1952* (Chicago: University of Chicago Press, 1961), *passim*, and Abram Bergson, *The Real National Income of Soviet Russia Since 1928* (Cambridge: Harvard University Press, 1961), *passim*.

very sensitive to particular methods employed and to "weights" utilized in their computation.[25]

The most thorough estimates of the Soviet real gross national product have been made by Professor Abram Bergson, who finds that it increased at the following average annual rates (in percentages): during the first two FYP's, from 1928 to 1937—4.8-11.9; 1950-1960—7.0; and for the entire period 1928-1960—4.5-6.3.[26] If we eliminate the six years by which, at the least, Soviet growth was set back by the war, the average annual rate for 1928-1960 was 5.5-7.7 per cent.[27] These are very high rates to be sustained over decades, but they have been equaled or surpassed in non-communist countries.[28] Since 1960, however, there has been a considerable slowdown in over-all Soviet growth, though it is still too soon to tell whether the trend is temporary or lasting.

As we might expect from our knowledge of Soviet priorities, industrial production grew more rapidly than the economy as a whole—by 9-10 per cent per annum during 1950-1960 (by Western recomputation),[29] though appreciably less than that since 1960. Within industry, the main emphasis has been consistently on its "heavy" branches, as perhaps well represented by the twenty-fold increase in the output of steel between 1928 and 1964.[30] Even faster has been the expansion of machinery output,[31] thus permitting very rapid accumulation of capital stock as well as extensive weapons production.

A contrasting picture is presented by agriculture. Following the severe setback during the collectivization drive, and another during World War II, and being continuously squeezed to provide resources for industrialization, agriculture barely recovered its 1928 level of output by the time of Stalin's death, and was still below the 1928 level per capita of the total population. And while a considerable injection of resources into this sector after 1953 succeeded in raising total output by about 50 per cent over the next five years, there has been very little advance since 1958. Once again, agriculture is a serious drag on the Soviet economy.

As for consumption levels, they, too, suffered severe setbacks during the early thirties and during the forties, rose rapidly for about five years after

[25] Cf. Campbell, op. cit., Chapter 6.

[26] Bergson, The Economics of Soviet Planning, p. 306. Where a range is given, the lower figure weights production increases by Soviet 1937 prices, the higher figure, by 1928 prices. The methodology of these estimates is rather complicated.

[27] Bergson deducts only the four war years and obtains 5.2-7.3 per cent.

[28] Of the major non-communist economies, by far the fastest growing in the postwar period has been Japan, averaging about 9 per cent per year during 1953-1963, or nearly the same as Yugoslavia.

[29] See Rush V. Greenslade and Phyllis Wallace in U.S. Congress, Joint Economic Committee, Dimensions of Soviet Economic Power (Washington, D.C.: Government Printing Office, 1962), pp. 115ff.; also, collation of official and estimated series on pp. 161-162, ibid.

[30] This averages 10 per cent per year for 30 years (omitting the six years mentioned in the preceding paragraph).

[31] Richard Moorsteen, weighting physical series by 1937 Soviet prices, found a 43-fold increase in civilian machinery output between 1928 and 1958; Prices and Production of Machinery in the Soviet Union 1928-1958 (Cambridge: Harvard University Press, 1960), p. 106.

Stalin's death, and have advanced much more slowly since. At present, the average is appreciably higher than in 1928,[32] though not so much because of greater per capita consumption of the basic goods—food, clothing, and hous- ing—as because of a very much larger supply of various other manufactured goods, including some durable consumer goods, medical services, education, recreation, and the like. Changed consumption patterns, and especially the in- tervening large-scale urbanization of the population, make it difficult to de- termine just how much higher consumption levels are now than in 1928. When a peasant moves to the city, his whole mode of life changes; he ceases to supply himself with many things and buys them in the shops and develops new needs. Under such conditions, monetary yardsticks become quite unreli- able. Nonetheless, it is quite clear that the Soviet consumer has so far partaken of only a small part of the increased productivity of the Soviet economy. It has been his prolonged privation—and, at times, starvation—that has helped transform the country from a relatively backward one into the second largest industrial power in the world.

Full communism, the society of abundance, is held up as the ultimate goal. We need not concern ourselves here with whether it will ever arrive— or in what form. The more immediate objective, much publicized by Mr. Khrushchev in the late fifties but little mentioned since the Soviet economy began slowing down (and the American economy, speeding up) in recent years, is to catch up with the United States in per capita production and consumption by 1970. The unlikeliness of this specific objective being attained need not blind us to the fact that the Soviet economy will probably continue to grow fast in the foreseeable future, even if not as fast as in the past decade.

FACTORS
BEHIND RAPID GROWTH

The most fundamental factor underlying the rapid growth of the Soviet economy has been undoubtedly the regime's determination to indus- trialize and amass military power as fast as possible, not hesitating to impose severe sacrifices on the population and to enforce its will through ruthless police control and terror. True, since Stalin's death police terror has been less in evidence and more attention has been paid to the consumer; but the de- termination to continue rapid industrialization remains.

More specifically, the Soviet Union has been devoting a large share of its resources to growth, year in, year out. Thus, the rate of investment (the ratio of gross investment to gross national product) has been around 25 per cent in "normal" times, rising to over 30 per cent by the 1960's—very high rates for a none-too-rich country which is simultaneously spending heavily

[32] For summary figures the reader is referred to Bergson, *The Economics of So- viet Planning,* p. 314, Table 13.5, which rests on meticulous investigations by Janet G. Chapman. Much analytical information on Soviet growth (including a study by Mrs. Chapman) will be found in Abram Bergson and Simon Kuznets (eds.), *Economic Trends in the Soviet Union* (Cambridge: Harvard University Press, 1963).

An extensive and well-rounded appraisal of the condition and accomplishments of the Soviet economy as of the end of 1965, written by a large number of American specialists, is to be found in U.S. Congress, Joint Economic Committee, *New Directions in the Soviet Economy* (Washington, D.C.: U.S. G.P.O., 1966), 5 volumes.

on military needs. In addition, large outlays on training, research, and similar activities have been made. (Official statistics claim that the number of professionals and trained technicians increased twenty-fold between 1928 and 1963.) Second, these resources have been purposefully (if not always efficiently) directed into the high-priority industries, those industries that underpin national power and produce the capital goods for further growth. By contrast, those industries that serve primarily private consumption, including housing, were for a long time relatively neglected. Third, advanced technology has been taken over from the advanced countries in the largest and most highly organized operation of this sort ever undertaken anywhere. Very large amounts of machinery and equipment have been imported from the West and, since World War II, also from the more advanced communist countries as a way of speeding capital formation and importing advanced know-how. Thousands of foreign technicians were brought to work in the Soviet Union in the twenties and thirties.

While these measures served to enlarge rapidly the stocks of physical capital, human skills, and technological knowledge, there was simultaneously a rapid expansion in the non-agricultural labor force. The main sources of this expansion have been the increment in the total working-age population, an absolute decline in the agricultural labor force, and the entry of many women into gainful employment outside agriculture. We should mention also that unemployment (not counting disguised unemployment among the peasants) disappeared soon after the FYP's began and the opposite problem, excessive hiring and hoarding of labor, made its appearance.

There is no mystery about the high growth rates of the USSR and other countries with Soviet-type economies. They are explainable by the factors just listed, and particularly by rapid increases in capital stock and in the non-agricultural labor force. The "dynamic efficiency" of Soviet growth apparently has not been especially high.[33] The most distinctive element in this record is the determined application of all the power of a totalitarian state to maximize its industrial might. Even so, the process was greatly facilitated by the country's relatively highly favorable population-resource ratio and by the considerable industrialization that had already taken place before the Revolution. With at least as much determination but lacking these two factors, Communist China has found it much more difficult to industrialize on the Soviet model, relying primarily on her own resources more than did Russia thirty years earlier.[34]

[34] For lack of space to trace the several major changes in the Chinese Communist economy, we limit ourselves here to refer the reader to the following books: T. J. Hughes and D. E. T. Louard, *The Economic Development of Communist China, 1949-1960*, 2nd edition (London: Oxford University Press, 1961); Choh-Ming Li (ed.), *Industrial Development in Communist China* (New York: Praeger paperback, 1961), and Alexander Eckstein, *Communist China's Economic Growth and Foreign Trade* (New York, McGraw-Hill, 1966). See also Richard T. Gill, *Economic Development: Past and Present,* this series, Chapter 6. Nor can we take up here the other communist economies outside of Eastern Europe—namely, North Korea, North Vietnam, Outer Mongolia, and Cuba.

OTHER EAST EUROPEAN
COUNTRIES

The establishment of Soviet hegemony in Eastern Europe at the end of World War II was quickly followed by the establishment of Soviet-style economies in Albania, Bulgaria, Czechoslovakia, East Germany, Poland, Rumania, and Yugoslavia. The Soviet institutional pattern and planning methods were copied down to the smallest detail. The process was essentially completed during the early 1950's, although the collectivization of the peasantry was fully accomplished—except in Poland and Yugoslavia—only toward the end of the decade. In Poland, as an immediate consequence of the political upheaval of 1956, the unpopular collective farms were mostly dissolved and agriculture reverted almost entirely to private farming. Otherwise, the Polish economy remains quite faithful to the Soviet model. The Yugoslav economy, which broke away from the Soviet model shortly after the country's political break with Moscow, is the subject of the following chapter.

Having taken over the Soviet economic system, the other countries of Eastern Europe also took over all of its strengths and problems. Industrial production and urbanization advanced very quickly.[35] By contrast, consumption standards advanced much more slowly, and sometimes not at all, while agricultural production lagged badly. The various operating problems that we have already taken note of in the Soviet case appeared in all the other Soviet-type economies as well. As in the USSR, economic growth tended to slow down markedly after 1960, especially in the more developed countries, such as Czechoslovakia. And various institutional reforms came to be advocated, and some adopted from 1963 on. We shall discuss these later in this chapter.

The USSR, and the other East European countries (excluding Yugoslavia and more recently Albania) and Outer Mongolia are members of the Council for Mutual Economic Assistance (CMEA, also often designated as *Comecon*). Their foreign trade has been mostly with one another since the later forties. But CMEA—formed in 1949 but largely inactive for most of the first decade—has lately been trying to go farther: to achieve coordination among the national medium-term plans and to bring about an efficient division of labor among its member countries. In this it has met with relatively little success owing to the technical difficulties of coordinating the planning and operation of command economies in the absence of a supranational Gosplan, the lack of meaningful prices in its area, and, more recently, a growing assertion of economic nationalism by some of the East European states (especially Rumania).[36]

---

[35] A summary of the official and Western-estimated rates of growth of industrial production in most East European countries up to 1960 may be found in Maurice Ernst, "Overstatement of Industrial Growth in Poland," *Quarterly Journal of Economics,* Vol. LXXIX, No. 4 (1965), pp. 623-641.

[36] Cf. Michael Kaser, *Comecon: Integration Problems of the Planned Economies* (London: Oxford University Press, 1965), and, more concisely, Andrzej Korbonski, "Comecon," *International Conciliation,* No. 549 (September, 1964).

COMMAND OR MARKET?

In the mid-1960's, despite an industrial capacity second only to that of the United States, the Soviet Union is still only partly industrialized by Western standards. At least one third of its labor force still works in agriculture; nearly half the population is still rural. Labor productivity, especially in agriculture, is but a fraction of what it is in America. So are consumption levels. Technologically, the Soviet economy is full of paradoxes—the very backward interspersed with the most advanced. The motorization of the country has hardly begun; a modern chemical industry is only now appearing. Many superb modern items, including space vehicles and guided missiles, are produced; yet, as a rule, the quality of most products is low, for reasons we have already stated. The economy functions at a low level of efficiency and often fails to satisfy the most elementary demands. The consumer, especially, expects much better of the economy than he is getting. The society is profoundly bureaucratized. The Communist party continues to rule at all levels, but it is now a conservative party in the sense that it acts to preserve existing patterns of power and privilege. There is considerable corruption, stealing from the state, short-changing the consumer, and deceiving superiors.

The waste and inefficiency of the Soviet economy and of its counterparts in Eastern Europe, and more recently the slackening of growth, have generated a vast critical and soul-searching literature, though all normally within the bounds of Marxist socialism. Many institutional reforms, big and little, but perforce always this side of capitalism, are proposed. The quest for improvement carries urgency, for the very growth and increasing sophistication of the economy render it progressively less amenable to planning and management on the Soviet model. Whatever the command economy's virtues in *mobilizing* resources for rapid industrialization, its high order of centralization seems to be ill-suited to the efficient operation of an industrialized—or even half-industrialized—country.

Micro-Economic Reform

Most of the problems of Soviet-type economies are micro-economic; they affect specific industries and goods—bottlenecks, low quality, wrong product-mix, resistance to innovation—although in the aggregate these "micro-" problems add up to a whale of a big one. Thus most proposals for reform have been aimed at micro-economic planning and management and advocated short-circuiting the very long lines of communication between buyer and seller by letting the two deal with each other directly rather than through a plethora of planning and administrative organs. But this would not be a simple change. It would require granting enterprises in all the Soviet-type economies much greater autonomy than they now possess to determine their output and input mixes, which in turn may require the dismantling of much of the system of **93** producer goods' allocation, a cornerstone of Soviet economic administration. Furthermore, it would require establishing a clear-cut objective for the firm, which almost certainly would be profit. Prices would have to be revised to permit buyer and seller to agree without compulsion from above, and also to render the profit-making meaningful from the standpoint of social goals. These goals would have to be set much more rationally and flexibly than hitherto, if not left "free" altogether. Management would have to be accorded new incentives to strive for profit for the enterprise and to undertake economically rational innovation. Such measures might amount to the introduction of a market mechanism in at least some areas of the command economy; at any rate, they would certainly amount to a considerable decentralization. Some small-scale activities even might be turned over to private enterprise— though any reversion to a more substantial capitalism is highly unlikely in the USSR and Eastern Europe in the foreseeable future. Planning would lose most of its concern with detail and would concentrate on rates and directions of development, specific programs, and macro-economic stabilization. Finance would gain in importance as an indirect way of steering the decentralized decisions into desired channels and keeping them under over-all control of the central authorities.

Ideas of this general sort have been increasingly advanced in the Soviet-style countries since the mid-fifties and sixties. The example of the Yugoslav market economy has no doubt played a major role in this regard, although many of the decentralizing proposals in the USSR and the other East European countries have been less far-reaching, more partial, and not always internally consistent. The term "Libermanism" is now commonly used in the West to refer generically to decentralizing ideas and schemes in the Soviet-type economies, especially those that would grant greater autonomy to the individual enterprise. The term refers to E. Liberman, a Soviet professor who has repeatedly advanced such (though relatively moderate) proposals.[37]

We have already had occasion to examine some of the issues inherent in any choice between centralization and decentralization in a formal organization;[38] they apply in the present instance as well. In addition, any decentralization raises some sticky politico-economic questions, such as to whom and how far shall decision-making power be delegated. After such delegation, planning would then lose most of its concern with detail and would concentrate on rates and directions of development, specific programs, and macro-economic stabilization. Finance, on the other hand, would gain in importance as a way of steering the decentralized decisions into desired channels and keeping them under over-all control.

Since 1963 numerous experiments have been conducted in East European countries, which involve tampering with forms of planning and management in the micro-economic sphere and which affect firms where supple response to demand is especially important—e.g., in the consumer goods or export industries. These experiments usually have assigned greater autonomy

[37] Cf. Alec Nove, "The Liberman Proposals," *Survey,* No. 47 (April, 1963), pp. 112-118. Translations of some of the relevant Soviet articles will be found in *Problems of Economics,* Vol. VIII, Nos. 2, 3, 4 (1965).
[38] See pp. 20 ff.

to the enterprise, enhanced the role of profit as a management goal, and sometimes allowed greater price flexibility. It is of course questionable whether a reform involving a whole system can be tested in only a few enterprises operating in an otherwise unchanged milieu. At any rate, such experiments have been followed by more extensive reform, as in East Germany in 1963, the very-far reaching one in Czechoslovakia, relatively mild ones in Poland and the USSR in 1965, and one in Hungary that appears to be imminent as this book goes to press in early 1966.[39]

It should not be inferred that there is considerable consensus in all the Soviet-style countries in favor of significant economic decentralization, if not "marketization." The reverse is true: There is strong opposition to the trend, and bitter struggles are revolving around this issue in every country. There are those who oppose decentralization because they believe that centralized management of the economy is superior, especially for rapid growth. But there are also many who oppose change for fear of losing positions of power and privilege and unleashing events that may be beyond political control. As we have already observed, where they rule the communist parties are conservative in addition to being strongly entrenched. And there are those who oppose decentralization because they adjudge the political climate not to be ripe for thoroughgoing marketization and are convinced that anything less is doomed to fail and to discredit the whole idea. They have a point. If the decentralization is only partial, it may fail to establish an effective market mechanism while robbing the command principle of its efficacy as well.

The question of decentralization of management and planning is of course intertwined with many others that are being intensely debated (though often still in Aesopian language): Whether the traditional communist emphasis on heavy industry should be relaxed and consumer goods favored more? Whether the rate of investment should be lowered so that consumers might start benefiting immediately as well? Or how to ensure employment for a rapidly expanding labor force as the rate of economic growth slackens.

Mathematizing Planning

Both decentralizers and centralists draw hope from the much-discussed prospect of using mathematical methods and electronic computers in planning. The centralists see mathematical planning models and computers as a way of ridding planning and management of its present slowness, crudity, and imprecision, while preserving their centralized nature and great detail. The economy would remain a command economy, but the commands would be decided swiftly and issued continually by machines on the basis of continuously arriving information. Moreover, the computers would be programmed to solve not only for mutual consistency of commands but also for efficiency

[39] The Czech reform is commented upon in footnote 16 of Chapter 7, while the Soviet reform is taken up in a later section of the present chapter. The interested reader will find much current discussion of the East European economic reforms in the monthly journal *East Europe* and in the bi-monthly *Problems of Communism*.

of resource use. While such a computerized command economy is theoretically conceivable, its realization in the foreseeable future in the communist countries is rather unlikely because of both insufficient development of mathematical economics and an as yet severe shortage of electronic "hardware."

The decentralizers, on the other hand, see mathematical methods and computers as helping to plan the broad directions of economic activity while leaving day-to-day operation to a socialist market mechanism, to solve specific problems of resource use and investment, and to compute rational prices. For this sort of thing there is already some precedent in the planning practice of *capitalist* market economies, as we have seen.

THE SOVIET REFORMS OF 1965

We have already taken note of one aspect of the Soviet reforms that were announced in September-October 1965—the abolition of sovnarkhozes and their replacement by reconstituted industrial ministries. The other aspect is the granting of somewhat greater autonomy to the industrial enterprise—i.e., some degree of decentralization. But unlike the creation of ministries, the decentralizing measures did not go into effect immediately; instead, they are to be gradually "phased in" by 1968, as is also the recalculation of prices in individual industries.

Even when completed—at least according to present indications—these measures will not amount to a major decentralization. The notorious gross value of output is to be replaced by value of sales as a major success indicator for the industrial firm in order to discourage the production of unsalable goods. Physical production targets will remain, but supposedly will be fewer in number (and probably more aggregative). Managers will have more power to determine the structure of the firm's inventories and the size and composition of the firm's labor force (though wage rates will remain centrally fixed and total payroll limits will be retained). (These provisions have in the past been much violated anyway.) Firms will begin paying interest on their assets to the state for the sake of more prudent management—a novelty that already had been introduced in most other East European countries in recent years. Prices will continue to be centrally fixed and materials will continue to be allocated (though a general intention to remove some producer goods from allocation was expressed). The success of the reform will largely hinge on how well prices approximate equilibrium levels and how well they express the goods' relative scarcities, and to what extent materials allocation will continue to shackle managers' freedom of action. Perhaps the most significant measure pertains to investment—namely, the intention to leave about one fifth of gross fixed investment to decentralized decision by enterprises in order to permit them to modernize and rationalize their operations. But how well this will function depends on many factors, including the nature of prices, the adequacy of incentives, and the availability of the necessary equipment and materials.

In sum, it is as yet difficult to appraise that aspect of the 1965 Soviet reform which pertains to decentralization because it will be carried out over several years—and could well be revised in either direction in the process.

SUMMARY

The Soviet economy is a socialist command economy with money, considerable freedom of household choice (but not household sovereignty), and detailed centralized planning. Much of the planning is coordinative, substituting for the absent market mechanism. Both sanctions and individual incentives are widely used to elicit compliance with plans and to spur productivity. The system is so organized—including the collectivization of agriculture—as to mobilize resources to the utmost, maintain a high rate of investment, and utilize modern technology in order to maximize the rate of growth. Preference in development has been going to heavy industry so as to enlarge rapidly the capacity for further capital formation and to maximize national power. After decades of neglect, agriculture and consumer goods are now receiving considerably more attention than before. This system succeeded in rapidly increasing industrial production—often with much waste and at the expense of variety, quality, and service—but has been lately showing signs (including a marked slowing down since 1960) of being too centralized and crude for the growing sophistication of the economy and the consumers' mounting aspirations. Improvement of the system, including the introduction of some elements of the market mechanism, are being widely and intensely discussed, and some significant reforms are under way.

The Socialist Market

Economy: Yugoslavia

CHAPTER SEVEN

THE EARLY THEORIZING

The idea that a socialist economy—one in which means of production are publicly owned—can also be a market economy was slow in maturing. Its intellectual origins lie, first, with those neoclassical economists of the late nineteenth and early twentieth centuries, mostly non-socialist, who insisted that the "economic problem," the best use of available resources for society's ends, was formally the same regardless of who owned the productive assets, and would be solved with the aid of prices, wages, the interest rate, and so on, under socialism as well as under capitalism. Second, they lie with those socialist economists of democratic inclination—in Germany, England, and the United States in the twenties and thirties—who were searching for a reply to the taunts from anti-socialist economists (the most famous being Ludwig von Mises) that socialism would be incapable of efficient resource allocation for lack of meaningful prices freely forming in the market.[1] The end result was the so-called "competitive solution," a *model* of a perfectly competitive socialist economy that, like the model of a perfectly competitive capitalist economy, achieved static efficiency by means of the market mechanism. In this model, individual socialist firms would compete with one another within a

[1] For an historical survey of these strands of socialist thought see Carl Landauer, *European Socialism: A History of Ideas and Movements,* Vol. II (Berkeley: University of California Press, 1959), pp. 1643f.

market economy, while the allocation of resources (except for the over-all rate of saving) would be ultimately determined via freedom of household choice.

The advocates of the competitive solution soon found themselves in a lively polemic not only with anti-socialists but also with more authoritarian socialists. To the latter, competition and the market mechanism represented everything that socialism has traditionally stood *against;* nor did they put much stock in consumer sovereignty. Instead, they preferred the "centralist solution," a close cousin to the planned, command economy that the USSR was introducing at the time.[2]

The advantages that, for instance, Oskar Lange in his celebrated essay [3] claimed for the model of the competitive socialist economy over its capitalist counterpart were these: (1) A more just distribution of income owing to the elimination of private property incomes, and for the same reason a more meaningful pattern of effective demand for consumer goods; (2) more opportunity to take account of externalities; and (3) stabilization of the economy at high employment by bringing the rate of saving into equality with the rate of investment. In Lange's model, a Central Planning Board sets prices so as to equate demand and supply, while the managers of individual socialist firms and industry planners push production of every good to the point where its marginal cost equals its price. This ensures that every unit of every resource is used to the maximum satisfaction of effective demand.

The rule for (static) efficiency—output where marginal cost equals price—had actually been developed by Abba P. Lerner, who in a major work [4] that appeared some years after Lange's essay, presented a model that differed from Lange's in at least two important respects. Lerner avoided price-setting by a Central Planning Board and instead left the process to the free market. Second, he stressed that private or public ownership mattered little from the point of view of allocative efficiency, except where subsidization was necessary on static efficiency grounds.

Yet the first socialist market economy to make its appearance in the real world following these debates [5]—that of Yugoslavia—developed quite

[2] A well-known analytical survey of the literature is Abram Bergson, "Socialist Economics" in Howard S. Ellis (ed.), *A Survey of Contemporary Economics* (Philadelphia: Blakiston [for the American Economic Association], 1948), pp. 412-448.

[3] "On the Economic Theory of Socialism" in Oskar Lange and Fred M. Taylor (Benjamin E. Lippincott, ed.), *On the Economic Theory of Socialism* (Minneapolis: University of Minnesota Press, 1938), pp. 99ff.

[4] *The Economics of Control* (New York: Macmillan, 1947). This is one of the most readable of the important economic treatises published in recent decades.

[5] Actually, there had already existed a workable socialist market economy before the debate reached its high watermark—the Soviet economy under the so-called New Economic Policy (NEP) from 1921 to 1928. Under the NEP, all large-scale economic activity was conducted by the state, agriculture was private, and there was some small-scale private enterprise in trade, manufacturing, and so on. The state exercised close over-all control over the whole economy, but the command principle even within the state sector was secondary to the market mechanism. The NEP was highly successful in achieving full recovery for the Soviet economy from its virtual paralysis in 1921. See V. N. Bandera, "The New Economic Policy (NEP) as an Economic System," *Journal of Political Economy*, Vol. LXXI, No. 3 (1963), pp. 265-279.

independently of this theorizing. Instead, it arose as a reaction to the country's earlier experience with the Soviet-type command economy.

YUGOSLAVIA

World War II brought a communist regime to Yugoslavia. However, unlike those in other East European countries, this regime was not imposed by the conquering Soviet Army but won its own victory in a most difficult war against many internal and external enemies. The victorious military leader and the president of the postwar government, Tito, proved to be too independent-minded for Stalin. The two fell out over who was to be boss within Yugoslavia and in June, 1948, broke completely with each other.

Until then the Yugoslavs had been second to none among the Soviet satellites in faithfully copying Soviet economic institutions and methods. The rift with Stalin gave them the opportunity to take a more detached look at the system they had only recently transplanted. They found it wanting on many scores: inefficient (as discussed in the preceding chapter), neglecting the consumer, overcentralized, overbureaucratized, and affording no opportunity for the individual worker to feel meaningfully involved in the production process. The last fault—"alienation"—had traditionally been one of the main charges thrown out against the capitalist economy by Marxists; it seemed incongruous that a socialist economy should suffer as much from it. Lastly, they found that the collectivization of agriculture was highly unpopular with the peasants and a fetter on farm production.

The distinctive economic system that Yugoslavia developed in the early fifties, after much trial and error, aims at a relatively high degree of decentralization of economic activity as a way of combating bureaucratization and affording maximum opportunity for producers' participation in economic decisions, while at the same time preserving its socialist aspects and speeding the development of what is still a relatively backward economy.[6]

OWNERSHIP
AND MANAGEMENT

After permission was given in 1953 to peasants already in collectives to leave them, the private sector in agriculture increased from three-fourths to over 90 per cent, measured in terms of arable land, later gradually declining to 87 per cent (in 1964). The remaining 13 per cent of arable land is occupied by state farms and collectives. Private farms are normally limited to 10 hectares (24.7 acres) in size, a substantial amount by Yugoslav stand-

[6] There is a now considerable body of writing in English on the Yugoslav economy, some of it originating in Yugoslavia. See especially George W. Hoffman and Fred Warner Neal, *Yugoslavia and the New Communism* (New York: Twentieth Century Fund, 1962); Albert Waterston, *Planning in Yugoslavia* (Baltimore: Johns Hopkins Press paperback, 1962); and Carl Landauer, *Contemporary Economic Systems* (Philadelphia: Lippincott, 1964), Chapter 20.

The author is grateful to Professors J. Sirotković (Zagreb) and Benjamin Ward for comments on this chapter. All responsibility remains with the author.

ards, but are otherwise not restricted in their operation. Private enterprise is also permitted in small-scale production and trade outside agriculture, though no more than five persons may be employed by a private employer (not counting family members).

With these exceptions, all enterprises are publicly owned, and it is in this "socialist sector" that one of modern Yugoslavia's most distinctive institutions—so-called *workers' management*—is found. The basic idea is that the workers (including white-collar employees) of an enterprise, though not its legal owners, have the ultimate authority for its affairs as well as a financial stake in the results of its operation. In this manner the old socialist ideal of industrial democracy is to be realized, the "alienation" of the worker from his place of work is to be minimized, and at the same time the constructive energies of the workers are to be enlisted for their own and the social good.

Of course, workers' management cannot be meaningful unless the enterprise itself enjoys a good deal of autonomy. In the Yugoslav case this is achieved by relating the firm to the economy by means of the market mechanism rather than by a Soviet-style command hierarchy. Within the individual enterprise, there is a management board consisting of the enterprise's own workers elected by and responsible to a workers' council, which in turn is elected by and responsible to the totality of the enterprise's employees. Day-to-day management is, however, up to a manager ("director"), who at once reports to the management board (of which he is a member) and overrules it in the event of conflict with law. He is hired and fired by procedures in which the interests of both the enterprise's management board and the local government ("commune") are represented.

In order to give the enterprise and the individual worker a powerful incentive to produce and to do so prudently and efficiently, the workers' earnings—according to rates set by each workers' council—come from the enterprise's net income. (Wages as such are no longer paid, though the state does guarantee certain minimum earnings.) A part of the enterprise's net income may be reserved at its own discretion (and with the encouragement of tax laws) for internal investment.[7]

Establishment of New Enterprises

If each enterprise is run by its workers, how can one come into existence before it has hired any workers? Sometimes, a new enterprise is "spun off" by an old one. Or a group of persons may band together to found a new enterprise, provided the initial capital can be raised from some governmental source. In the case of major, important new ventures, the initiative may come from the federal or republic (state) government, which would also advance the necessary funds. But most commonly the impulse comes from the local commune which may have one or more motives to establish a new enterprise:

[7] For a discussion and appraisal of the system of workers' management see, in addition to the works cited in the preceding note, Benjamin Ward, "Workers' Management in Yugoslavia," *Journal of Political Economy,* Vol. LXV, No. 5 (1957), pp. 373-386; and Adolf Sturmthal, *Workers Council* (Cambridge: Harvard University Press, 1964), Chapters 4 and 8.

fiscal (since the profits of enterprises are a major source of revenue for the communes), to relieve local unemployment, to supply the commune's population with needed goods or services, and even for sheer prestige. In this case, the initial capital comes from resources at the commune's disposal and from various investment banks and government funds.

THE MARKET

The Yugoslav market mechanism operates along familiar lines, though it must be remembered that it is national planning that steers it in the desired direction. In its choice of outputs, inputs, technology, and investment, the individual enterprise is guided primarily by the prospect of net income. With the important qualification to be presently noted, prices fluctuate in response to supply and demand. There is also a capital market; that is, enterprises borrow from banks and other institutions, for both short-run and long-run purposes, subject to interest charges and other financial terms.

Being a market economy, the Yugoslav economy is subject to virtually all the hazards and problems of one. Thus, there is an ever-present danger of monopoly with the undesirable effects of high prices for consumers, excessive earnings by the *workers* of the monopolistic enterprise (and, one might add, by the local commune), and misallocation of resources. This danger is greatly enhanced by the fact that the country is relatively small and cannot afford too many firms in industries with important economies of scale, while competition from abroad may be ineffective because of the chronic shortage of foreign exchange to pay for imports. While fully cognizant of the problem, the Yugoslav authorities have not yet taken very determined steps to combat monopoly and other restrictions on competition.

Another serious problem has been presented by strong inflationary pressure, a concomitant of the rapid economic expansion. In order to contain it, the authorities have frequently seen fit to resort (among other measures) to extensive price control. Whatever its advantages for combating inflation and its effects, price control interferes with the operation of the market mechanism, throws demand and supply out of balance, and tends to distort the direction of investment. These effects prompt additional controls and the decentralized nature of the whole system is thus threatened. However, price control is generally regarded in Yugoslavia as an emergency measure and not, as in the USSR, a permanent feature of the system.[8]

Labor Market; Unemployment

Owing to the system of workers' management, the labor market in Yugoslavia contains some distinctive features. Since there are nominally no wages,

[8] During 1963-1965, a policy favoring reduction of central economic controls has been in the ascendance, despite mounting inflationary pressure. In July 1965, all price ceilings were sharply raised and the Yugoslav monetary unit, the dinar, was devalued by 40 per cent in the hope of stabilizing prices at the new levels and thus eventually minimizing controls and proceeding with the further decentralization. The success of this drastic measure clearly depends in large part on avoiding a recurrence of inflationary pressure in the future.

there is also no formal price for labor; but workers are obviously guided in their choice of jobs by earning prospects in different enterprises. On the demand side, enterprises may tend to take on too few additional workers so as to avoid spreading their net incomes too thin; [9] they may also be reluctant to fire employees even when economically advisable because this may create awkward problems with the worker-managed firms.

The existence of workers' management in a socialist economy does not rule out conflicts of interest between minorities and majorities within enterprises, or between enterprises and society as a whole. Probably no economic system ever can, even under more affluent and democratic conditions than obtain in Yugoslavia. This raises the problem of trade unions and strikes. At first glance it may seem that there is no place for either in a system of workers' management. But in fact, labor unions do exist in Yugoslavia and are nationally fairly important, though wage bargaining with individual enterprises is not one of their significant functions. Rather, on the plant level they sometimes handle the grievances of individual workers or groups of workers. On the national level, they have been in recent years pressing hard with some success for an increase in the share of national income allotted to private consumption. There are also occasional strikes—though not conducted by unions—that are aimed by workers against their own managements or by whole enterprises against the central authorities (since the latter, despite the high order or economic decentralization, do affect the fortunes of enterprises through control of taxes, prices, and investment funds).

There has been appreciable unemployment in Yugoslavia in the face of chronic inflationary pressure. Much of it is "structural," occasioned by the difficulty of absorbing large numbers of village migrants who often lack the requisite skills.

PLANNING
AND STABILIZATION

Planning in Yugoslavia is much more similar to that in France than to that in the USSR, although in the relative extent of its publicly owned sector it is much closer to the latter than to France. The crucial consideration, however, is not "socialism" but the degree of decentralization in the economic system; i.e., the existence of a market economy. But, as in any market economy, short-range stabilization of employment and, especially, prices is also an important concern in Yugoslav policy.

Despite rapid growth in recent years, Yugoslavia is still a relatively poor and predominantly rural country, with economic (and cultural) contrasts that are as striking as in any other European country. The north exists on a Central European level of industrialization and wealth; the south is still on a

---

[9] Cf. Benjamin Ward, "The Firm in Illyria: Market Syndicalism," *American Economic Review,* Vol. LXVI, No. 4 (1958), pp. 373-386.

"Balkan" level. Ever since the end of World War II, the communist regime's primary goal has been to industrialize and modernize the country, and especially its backward regions, speedily and within a socialist framework. Since the early fifties, this framework has been the distinctive one that we have been describing in the present chapter.

Consequently, in drawing up the five-year plans, Yugoslavia's leaders and planners have striven for very high rates of over-all and (particularly) industrial growth, rising technological levels, a rapidly increasing standard of living, and—not the least—preferential development of the backward regions. A corollary objective has been the maintenance of very high rates of investment out of the national product. There are also annual plans with essentially similar goals.

The drive for development—and it has been very strong—comes from several sources. The government and the Communist party (known as the League of Communists of Yugoslavia) propagate an industrializing ideology. Moreover, the federal government and those of the separate republics invest directly in "social overhead" capital (e.g., roads, major public utilities) and initiate or suggest other investment projects to be undertaken at lower levels. Much initiative also comes from the enterprises themselves and (as we have seen) from communes. Until 1964, some 25-30 per cent of the funds going into fixed investment came from internal sources of enterprises, though even this portion was in large measure under effective control of the central authorities through a system of joint financing. The 70-75 per cent that came from the government or the banks originated primarily with the federal authorities and was of course derived largely from taxation. Thus Yugoslavia's high rate of investment has been largely tax financed. Since 1964, the banking system and investment financing have been considerably decentralized, the direct control of the central authorities over individual projects has been sharply reduced, and more reliance is coming to be placed on the internal resources of enterprises for financing investment.

In order to maintain the planned directions of development, centrally controlled investment funds have been allocated to individual industries and regions, for which the individual enterprises and communes then compete. Other instruments are also, of course, at the disposal of the authorities to the same ends: variations in prices, taxes, tariffs, and the rationing of foreign exchange.

However, much of the attention of Yugoslav authorities has been devoted to persistent short-range problems, such as a shortage of foreign exchange and inflationary pressure, which in turn have been in part occasioned by high demand on both the investment and the consumption sides. As we have already seen, this problem has led to rather extensive use of price controls, with negative effects on the proper operation of the market mechanism. But other disinflationary means have also been employed from time to time, such as limiting the lending power of banks, restraining consumer credit, and blocking a part of the liquid resources of enterprises.[10]

[10] The last-named measure bears a certain similarity to the Swedish system of investment reserves; see p. 68.

SUMMARY AND APPRAISAL

Since the early fifties, Yugoslavia has developed a highly distinctive economic system—a socialist market economy with workers' management and planned economic growth—which, though far from perfect, is clearly workable and possesses some marked advantages over the Soviet-type system. Among the latter we may list: (1) thanks to the market mechanism, better and faster mutual adjustment of demand and supply, greater attention to the needs of the consumer within the limits of resources allotted to consumption, and much wider scope to local economic initiative (whether by the enterprise or by the commune); (2) correspondingly, much lesser administrative pressure by the authorities on all facets of economic activity, as well as more relaxed (though still authoritarian) political control over the society in general; (3) avoidance of the oppressive and wasteful system of collectivized farming; and (4) a significant measure of industrial democracy within the socialist enterprises. Welfare-state measures have been introduced on a considerable scale.

But there are also many problems, as we have repeatedly noted. Many of them derive at bottom from the backwardness of the country and from the great contrasts among its regions. As a result—and given the governing ideology—it has been found necessary to reserve strong central controls in order to maintain high rates of investment, to limit consumption, and to favor the development of the more backward regions. National purposes and decentralized interests and initiative have often conflicted (as of course they do in other systems, too). For these reasons, as well as because of the novelty of the whole system, there have been numerous and frequent revisions of institutions and policies, which have added both to the problems of the economy and to the difficulty of appraising its merits and weaknesses.

On the whole, the Yugoslav regime has not been too doctrinaire in economic matters, compared with other communist regimes. And although it has permitted small-scale private enterprise even outside of agriculture, it has also tended to restrict its operation by taxes and other means so that the supply of many goods and services has been impaired to the inconvenience of the consumer.

Growth

One of the most striking recent achievements of the Yugoslav economy has been its extremely fast growth, among the very fastest in the world. Between 1954 and 1964, according to official statistics, the gross national product [11] increased almost 2½ fold, or 9.4 per cent per year; industrial production, 3¼ fold, or 12.5 per cent per year; agricultural output, by 60 per cent, or

[11] Like the other communist countries, Yugoslavia defines the gross national product as comprising *material* production only—that is, exclusive of final services.

almost 5 per cent per year.[12] Personal consumption also has increased sharply. Among the factors that explain this impressive record are: the high rate of investment; the direct initiative of the central authorities in carrying out capital formation plus the strong decentralized drive for investment (as already mentioned); and the large flow of labor to the cities from the villages, where it is in surplus.[13] One must also mention substantial foreign aid: $2.25 billion from the United States up to mid-1964,[14] and a smaller but substantial amount from other Western governments and from international institutions.

Workers' Management

That the institution of Yugoslav workers' management "works" is evident from the foregoing. But it is far from clear how close it comes to its own ideal of industrial democracy. In theory, management is ultimately responsible to the workers, and major policy decisions in each socialist enterprise are made by the workers' councils. All this is made possible by the autonomy of the enterprise within a market-economy context. Yet many questions remain. To what extent is the manager actually responsible to the workers' council, given the methods of his appointment and removal? In any case, in the larger enterprises, does not the power really lie with some "insiders"? And if power is in fact broadly diffused among the workers, how competent are they in such a relatively backward country to exercise it well? [15] But in Yugoslavia there is also the specific question of the influence of the League (party) of Communists. The party apparently does not as a rule interfere directly in the affairs of the individual enterprise, but it also can and probably does frequently exert influence through key personnel, trade unions, the commune government, and other channels.

The Yugoslav system is significant not only by virtue of its distinctiveness but also—perhaps even more so—because it serves as a living and workable model of an alternative socialist system for the Soviet-type economies of Eastern Europe. As such it exercises a great deal of attraction, though for many years Moscow-style communists tried hard to pretend it did not exist.[16]

[12] In the case of agricultural output, the base for our figures is the average level of 1953-1955.

[13] Between the census of March 1953 and that of March 1961, the urban population of Yugoslavia increased from 3,145,000 to 5,242,000, or by two-thirds, and as a percentage of the total population, from 18.5 per cent to 28.2 per cent. Over the same eight years, the number employed in industry and mining almost doubled.

[14] Of this amount, $188 million was in economic assistance loans, $386 million in grants, $696 million in military assistance, $874 million under the "Food for Peace" (Public Law 480) program, and $105 million in Export-Import Bank loans.

[15] Notice that some of these questions have their counterparts in regard to stockholders' control in capitalist corporations. By way of mental exercise, the reader may wish to compare and contrast the relations between the Yugoslav enterprises and their workers and capitalist corporations and their stockholders, in theory and practice.

[16] In January 1965, Czechoslovakia—which until then had one of the most rigid Soviet-style command economies in Eastern Europe—adopted a series of measures which, if realized, would have the effect of dismantling much of the command system and replacing it by a fairly extensive market mechanism. She was led to such a drastic reform by grave economic difficulties in the several preceding years. As yet, the Czech reform is still largely on paper; whether and how it will be carried out cannot yet be determined. In November, 1965, the Hungarian regime expressed its intention to carry out a reform which is rather similar to the Czech reform. It, too, is largely on paper so far.

CHAPTER EIGHT

THE INDIVIDUAL AND SOCIETY

Economic systems are for people. Even the most Stalinist communists do not openly deny it. (In the days of the greatest terror and privation under Stalin, his propaganda machine never ceased to proclaim how many benefits the regime had brought to the Soviet people!) The issues of market against command, centralization or decentralization of economic processes, planning or no planning and what kind of planning, controls and what kind of controls—either directly or indirectly these questions inevitably bear on the fundamental issue of the relationship between the individual or the group, on the one hand, and the larger group, the society, and the state of which they form a part, on the other hand.

We shall dwell briefly on two of the main aspects of this issue: (1) the individual's freedom and dignity within the economic (and political) order, and (2) harmonization of the individual's (or economic unit's) incentives and actions with the objectives of the larger group or of the society as a whole.

Individuality and Freedom

The individual's freedom and dignity within the economic order is in large measure a function of the alternatives open to him for his own deciding. Even if his decision is virtually predetermined by economic circumstances, as is a poor man's spending much of his income on basic food, the mere fact that he has at least some options contributes to the upholding of his individuality. (Anyone who has eaten Army rations for many months would most probably agree!) At least as important is the freedom of choice of job—and perhaps even more, the freedom to quit a job. Little wonder then that all the three main types of economic systems we have examined—the advanced capitalist, the Soviet, and the Yugoslav—share the institution of freedom of household choice, although they do differ fundamentally regarding the individual's place in society. The impairment of this freedom of choice as regards both the job (and place of residence) and consumption was among the more resented features of Stalinism, and the peasants' virtual attachment to collective farms is still greatly resented.

Freedom of operating one's own business or farm falls in the same category; and even if most people in an advanced economy would not and could not do so, the substantial existence of such opportunities in itself adds to the quality of the economic and social order. In any case, the tendency toward private enterprise is not easily stamped out even by protracted indoctrination and outright prohibition, as the experience of the Soviet Union demonstrates, and measures to enforce such prohibition only add to the tensions between the individual and the state. The Yugoslavs have done better by allowing a substantial if strictly circumscribed safety valve for the exercise of private enterprise.[1]

But most individuals in the advanced economies are not their own bosses; instead, they are employed, usually by large private or public organizations. They must confront other large and powerful organizations in addition to their employers: labor unions, professional associations, and especially the state at its several levels and in its many manifestations. In this environment the individual's or (minority's) protection at bottom rests probably on nothing more tangible than the acceptance of the democratic spirit and rules of the game by all concerned. But proper institutions help to hold up this slender reed. In one well-informed opinion the following are the minimal requirements of a "democratic industrial society":

—there should be as many power centers as possible, consistent with the effective functioning of society;
—these power centers should be roughly balanced in strength and should be independent of one another;
—the participants in each power center (i.e., union members, stockholders) should be able to exert at least a minimum of control over the leadership;
—each power center should have an adequate judicial system (grievance machinery) to protect the rights of the participants;
—necessary government controls in the economy should be concentrated on procedures rather than on substantive issues; e.g., instead of regulating prices or wages the government should seek to regulate mergers or the process of collective bargaining.[2]

[1] As we mentioned in Chapter 6, in Poland, too, agriculture has been almost wholly returned to private operation following the political events of 1956.

[2] Clark Kerr, "An Effective and Democratic Organization of the Economy," *in* The American Assembly, The President's Commission on National Goals, *Goals for Americans* (Englewood Cliffs: Prentice-Hall paperback, 1960), pp. 149-162. (The whole volume is a convenient collection of the objectives of what might be called the "mainstream" of informed American opinion of its time.) See also the works by Kerr *et al.* cited in Chapter 1, note 14.

(We might add to the last that government should prefer macro-economic over micro-economic planning and indirect over direct controls, when consistent with the attainment of social objectives.) We have already referred to the political case for private property (capitalism);[3] namely, that within certain bounds it represents a decentralization of the economy and contributes to the dispersion of power in society. Whether it is so in relation to such ideal societies as the Jeffersonian yeoman democracy or utopian communistic communities, it is clearly so in comparison with the Soviet-type economy or even the in-between Yugoslav type. Which is not to say that very much does not remain to be done to distribute power more widely even in the Western democracies.

Lastly, basic protection against risks of economic instability (e.g., unemployment) or personal misfortune (e.g., sickness) through private insurance or social security enlarges the individual's range of effective choice and enables him to assert his individuality.

Harmonizing Particular Acts with Social Objectives

Division of labor in the economy necessarily raises the question of harmony between the economic acts of individuals (economic units, agents), on one hand, and the objectives of the larger organization or the whole society, on the other. (For the moment, we take the nature of the objectives of the larger organization or of the society and the political process that determines them as given.) The problem is obviously of crucial importance in a market economy, capitalist or Yugoslav-style, where the individual economic unit is accorded considerable autonomy of deciding and acting. But in fact, as we have already glimpsed, it is perhaps of even greater importance in the Soviet-type command economy, owing to the greater demands placed by the organized society on the individual and economic unit while denying a socially constructive role to the individual's natural acquisitive tendencies.

Laissez faire is dead. We no longer assume, if we ever did, that the unhampered activity of every private economic unit brings about the best of all possible worlds. The market mechanism is not faultless and the modern state—itself far from infallible—intervenes in a myriad of ways (as we saw in Chapters 4 and 5): to take care of externalities, to regulate monopoly, to forbid outright many acts that are deemed to clash with the public interest, to stimulate other activities, to redistribute income and wealth after the market has done its distributing, and at times even to ration scarce goods in accordance with social priorities and to engage in outright production. But, everything considered, there is still a basic presumption in the market economy of lack of conflict between the particular lawful act of an economic unit and the public interest.[4]

For this presumption to be valid, three conditions must be met. First,

---

[3] *Supra,* Chapter 1, section on "extra-economic criteria."

[4] For a clear and non-technical statement of the basically technical problems of control under decentralization in large organizations (of which the market economy is a conspicuous instance) see Kenneth J. Arrow, "Control in Large Organizations," *Management Science,* Vol. 10, No. 3 (April, 1964), pp. 397-408.

the unit's objective(s) must be in harmony with society's objective(s). In a market economy, the most common objective of the individual firm is profit (though, as we have seen, it would be wrong to think of at least the larger firms as being straight profit maximizers). Since profit is the difference between value produced and value used up, it is thus the first approximation to net value created. And since increasing net value created comes very close to increasing the national income, which is what all societies desire, profit-making is therefore (in principle) usually assumed to be a socially legitimate objective for the individual economic unit in a market economy.[5]

This is also why nearly all of the proposals for reform of the Soviet-type system aim to supplant value of output by profit as the socialist firm's "success indicator." As the Soviet economy has learned from bitter experience, to downgrade profit is to upgrade waste. The old radical slogan "production for use and not for profit!" turned out to be a fallacy—because in an economy with highly developed division of labor almost the only way in which the dispersed economic agents can tell what is more useful is by seeing what is more profitable. Interestingly, the slogan of those reformers in the USSR who would upgrade the resource-allocative role of profitability in the Soviet economy is: "What is advantageous for society must be made advantageous also for the enterprise!"

Yet the converse does not necessarily hold; what is profitable for the enterprise need not be advantageous for society, either under capitalism or under socialism. Whether it does depends not only on the objectives but also on whether the prices that enter into the economic decisions approximate the relative scarcities of goods at the optimum, always bearing in mind that scarcities themselves are relative to the uses (goals) to which society wishes to put its resources. This, then, is the second condition. But we should also bear in mind that the ideal of price theory, efficient allocation of resources, need not be the ideal of the statesman or citizen, who may be willing to sacrifice some efficiency—in any case never completely attainable—for such other desiderata as growth, distributive equity, and the other values enumerated in Chapter 1.

And third, each economic resource must be under some decision-maker's (economic agent's) charge—though not necessarily direct ownership—who, in a decentralized system, must be induced to take the desired actions. The matter is trivial in an owner-managed firm; here profits (insofar as not taxed away) are both the measure of success and the inducement for action. It is different where ownership and management are effectively separated, as in many large capitalist corporations, in nationalized enterprises, in Soviet-style firms (to the extent they may act on their own), and in worker-managed Yugoslav firms. In these cases, managers must be either fully culturally conditioned to take the expected decisions,[6] or be given an incentive in the form of a share in the net benefits (or losses) resulting from his decisions, or both. The sharing out of a part of net income among workers as well as managers in

---

[5] The reader is reminded of the distinction between profit-*making* by enterprises and profit-*taking* by owners, on which more presently.

[6] Such cultural conditioning of managers, as well the industriousness of the labor force, are among the most important assets of the more highly industrialized societies. One effect is to reduce the productivity and efficiency implications of the ownership of industry—i.e., whether private or public.

Yugoslav enterprises and the profit-tied bonuses and profit-sharing plans in capitalist corporations of course strive to accomplish just this. The principle of inducement to action by society's sharing the benefits with the individual decision-maker is the same in all systems, even if the specific institutions that realize it are markedly different. (For many years now the Soviets have been struggling with the problem of appropriate rewards to managers and engineers for introducing economically beneficial innovations, although by law they are enjoined to do so anyway.)

CONVERGENCE?

The three major economic systems we have examined in this book arose in response to the challenges of industrialization and industrialism. Though they may have closer-range goals, such as military capability and national power, they all strive for material abundance based on modern technology. Is it likely that they will grow increasingly similar? Will some sort of relatively uniform "industrial society" emerge eventually? The question of "convergence" of the different economic (and political) systems has been receiving increasing attention in recent years.

Let us mention, first, that the very idea of convergence is abhorrent to those on the extremes of the ideological spectrum. Or, to be more exact, they speak in terms of the "submergence" of the *other* system, not a convergence of two or more.[7] Thus, the official Soviet position asserts that talk of "convergence" and of a uniform "industrial society" is just another anti-communist propaganda trick to divert attention from the inevitable, ultimate victory of communism throughout the world. "We shall bury you," is the way Mr. Khrushchev put it.[8] And there are some in the capitalist world who aver that socialism and communism are inherently so evil and unworkable that it is only a matter of time before the communist regimes collapse and their countries revert to capitalism. In other words, communism will "bury itself," perhaps with a little assist from the outside. So much for "submergence."

Now, of course, there is a good deal to the convergence theory. Industrialism and its concomitants—such as urbanization, widespread education and technical competence, higher consumption levels—impose their stamp on outlooks, values, behavior patterns, and even forms of economic organization. As the economy grows more complex, technology more sophisticated, and the consumer's needs more demanding—and as at the same time the need for brute mobilization of resources becomes less pressing—the market mech-

---

[7] The distinction between "submergence" and "convergence" in this context has been introduced by Zbigniew Brzezinski and Samuel P. Huntington, *Political Power: USA/USSR* (New York: Viking, 1964), pp. 419f., which is a thorough review of the convergence theory. The same analysis is presented in their article, "America & Russia: Converging Nations?" *Columbia University Forum* (Winter, 1964), pp. 12-17.

[8] Even in this intransigence, Mr. Khrushchev revealed himself to be the revisionist in international affairs that the Chinese Communists accuse him of being. Marx would have said of capitalism that it will bury *itself*.

anism becomes ever more attractive in relation to command. Ideological fervor flags with the passage of generations and as life grows more comfortable. It is thus not impossible that the other Soviet-type economies will, sooner or later, follow the examples of Yugoslavia, and now Czechoslovakia,[9] and will "marketize" themselves. But, as we stated at the end of Chapter 6, there is powerful opposition to "marketization" in these countries.

But if command is apt to give way to the market mechanism during the process of industrialization, the latter is also likely to yield everywhere more and more to social control for the sake of ensuring stability, providing public services, and directing economic development in socially desired ways. In the past, these kinds of planning and steering were instituted too rigidly in the East and perhaps too loosely in the West; some future convergence on this plane is not at all unlikely. (The already-mentioned considerable similarity between French and Yugoslav planning may be a case in point; they are, so to say, on the frontiers of capitalism and socialism, respectively.)

Another plane on which the systems are likely to move closer is that of the welfare state: protection of the individual against various personal risks, including illness, and broad provision of such services as education. The passage by the United States Congress in July, 1965, of a system of health insurance for elderly persons under federal social security (so-called Medicare) considerably reduces the gap between this country and other industrial countries in the field of social insurance.[10]

The process of convergence is likely to be slowest in those areas that are closest to the core of ideology and the essence of political power. To explain: In the West, private property under a measure of social control is widely accepted, while the nationalization issue is losing much of its ideological charge among both socialists and anti-socialists (except in the U.S.). This is part of an alleged process of growing pragmatism in Western industrial society—the "end of ideology" as some have called it. But while the advantages of nationalizing large-scale enterprises are dubious, the advantages of private enterprise in small-scale businesses are quite evident to anyone without ideological blinkers. And yet there is little sign that the communist regimes are prepared to make much of a concession in this area in the foreseeable future beyond what has already been conceded in Yugoslavia and Poland.

The other instance relates to political power and the closely related issue of industrial democracy. In the West, the advent of strong labor unions has tended to distribute power more broadly, at times even to send the pendulum in the other direction. There is no sign that Soviet-type communist regimes are prepared to stop using labor unions as instruments of their own power and chance the unions' independence. (In Yugoslavia, however, the national trade union organization has developed into a distinct political factor within

[9] On the Czechoslovak reforms of early 1965, see Chapter 7, note 16.

[10] While social insurance and public relief measures, especially before Medicare, have been narrower in range than in some European "welfare states" and rather uneven among individual states, the *amount* of assistance provided to recipients under separate programs compares very favorably with other countries. For analyses of this and other aspects of American welfare policies see, for example, Dorothy Wilson, "America and the Welfare State," Political and Economic Planning (P.E.P.), *Planning,* Vol. XXVI, No. 438 (25 January, 1960), 35 pp.; and Margaret S. Gordon, "U.S. Welfare Policies in Perspective," *Industrial Relations,* Vol. 2, No. 2 (February, 1963), pp. 33-61.

the framework of the communist regime.) Equally opposed, and for similar reasons, are the Soviet-type regimes to the establishment of autonomous workers' councils on the Yugoslav model. In sum, dictatorships cannot afford to permit the rise of meaningful social pluralism—though they cannot always thwart it—and having eliminated the independent power that comes with private property, they are most wary of the potentially independent power of workers' organizations. Whether they will succeed in suppressing it indefinitely, time will tell. But we may assume that convergence is less likely on the political than on the economic planes, and on the latter, the less likely the closer it comes to the core of political power.[11]

LOOKING AHEAD—
RICH AND POOR

While the Soviet-style East moves towards less rigid economic control by central authorities, and while the West is searching for more effective forms of social control and direction of the economy, both sides are beginning to look forward seriously to the problems of higher productivity. To be sure, most of the communist East, even omitting the communist countries of Asia, is still very far from abundance, still very poor by Western standards, and still struggling to provide adequate food and shelter for its populations. Nonetheless, the problems of forthcoming automation of production (only beginning there) and its effects on employment, of the direction in which mass consumption (still in its infancy there) should go when it comes, of public versus private services, and so forth, are being increasingly and perhaps not prematurely discussed by Soviet and other East European economists.

Much more pressing are the problems of increasing affluence and approaching abundance in the West. It may be paradoxical to speak of the problem of abundance in the United States while the country is mounting a "War on Poverty," but actually it is the realization of potential abundance that makes the persistent pockets of poverty both economically and politically intolerable. Clearly, we shall have to do much re-thinking of our institutions and values as the economy's productivity continues to grow at a sound pace. Already we are devising new techniques—mostly new forms of partnership or cooperation between the federal government, private industry, and the autonomous universities—in various frontier areas of technology and production, such as atomic energy, space exploration, and the use of artificial satellites for communication.

[11] The evolution of each *political* system in its own way rather than convergence, despite certain growing economic similarities, is the thesis of Brzezinski and Huntington; see their works cited in footnote 7. Jan Tinbergen's "Do Communist and Free Economies Show a Converging Pattern?" *Soviet Studies*, Vol. XII, No. 4 (April, 1961), pp. 333-341, leans more on the side of convergence; he is answered by Knud Erik Svendsen, "Are the Two Systems Converging?", *Øst-Økonomi*, No. 3 (December, 1962), pp. 195-209. See also Peter Wiles, "Will Capitalism and Communism Spontaneously Converge?" *Encounter* (June, 1963), pp. 84-90.

Should we de-emphasize sheer production growth and concentrate on shifting resources in favor of the public sector in order to redress the balance between "private affluence and public squalor," as John K. Galbraith has forcefully argued? [12] Or should the U.S. do the redressing while simultaneously forcing greater economic growth, because growth strengthens America for both internal and international tasks, as the Swedish economist Gunnar Myrdal has countered? [13] Should the federal government guarantee a substantial minimal income to every citizen regardless of what he contributes to production, because abundance will enable it and the need for markets require it? [14] Above all, how shall we, as individuals and as a society, make sure that the increased outpouring of material goods and the lengthening hours and years of leisure become a blessing and not a curse? What are the implications for our political and economic systems, our ideologies, our ethics, our myths, and our politics?

Most of the world's countries and people are far removed from such worries. They face the real "economic problem"—how to make do with scanty resources and how to increase them at a pace that is not intolerably slow. Few are the underdeveloped countries that have not expressed their intention to industrialize and develop, but their industrializing ideologies and the institutions they use or intend to use for the purpose vary greatly. The various economic systems in the advanced countries present themselves as models of industrialization. Yet we can expect only very few to opt definitely for either the "Western" (let alone the strictly American) economic system, or, outside the communist world, for the Soviet system, or, for that matter, for the Yugoslav model (though it has elicited some interest in a few underdeveloped countries).

To begin with, capitalism has a bad name to many people in the underdeveloped countries. It is associated in their minds with colonialism, imperialism, great differences in income and wealth, class tensions, lack of national solidarity, and so on. Others may dislike it precisely because of its association with political democracy. At least the phraseology if not the policy of many underdeveloped countries is thus anti-capitalist, although in some instances socialism is preached while capitalism is being effectively practiced (e.g., in India). In some cases "socialism" is simply a fashionable euphemism for political dictatorship. But the fact remains that, call it socialism or controlled (planned) capitalism, the role of the state in most of these economies is likely to be relatively high, if only because domestic private interests are likely to be too weak to accumulate the capital and to foster the industrialization that the political leaders (and often the population at large) deem required. On our part, it behooves us little to insist that the underdeveloped country copy our own institutions of industrial capitalism as closely as possible when their conditions and values are usually radically different from those we encountered and espoused in the nineteenth century.

[12] *The Affluent Society.*
[13] *Challenge to Affluence* (New York: Pantheon Books, 1963). See also his *Beyond the Welfare State* (New Haven: Yale University Press, 1960).
[14] Robert Theobald, "Abundance: Threat or Promise," *The Nation,* May 11, 1963. See also his *The Challenge of Abundance* (New York: Potter, 1961; Mentor paperback, 1962).

But while usually assigning a large role to the state and to economic planning, the non-communist underdeveloped countries are not copying the Soviet—or, for that matter, the Chinese—model of industrialization, either. For some it is unpalatable because of its attendant political repression and human sacrifice. For others it is unfeasible because their regimes could not institute the political controls implicit in the model even if they wanted to. For many it is irrelevant, because even with Soviet-style political controls they could not achieve anything like the Soviet rates of growth in view of their backwardness and lack of resources. Of the last, some may be watching Communist China's progress, which is still very much in the balance. Theirs are the really hard choices to make; they can use not only our example and our help but also our understanding.[15]

[15] The writing on economic development is by now enormous. For an eloquent analysis of the relation between economic development and choice of political system see Robert L. Heilbroner, *The Great Ascent: The Struggle for Economic Development in Our Time* (New York: Harper & Row, 1963; Torchbook paperback, 1963); and his *The Making of Economic Society* (Englewood Cliffs: Prentice-Hall paperback, 1962), Chapter 7.

Selected Readings

Not much is written on economic subjects that in one way or another is not relevant to the study of economic systems. Clearly, one must be very selective. On the other hand, there are so many good and germane books now available in paperback form, including many of those cited in this work, that it is possible to build up a decent library in the field with a few visits to bookstores and a relatively modest outlay of cash.

The reader is invited to follow up the numerous references in our footnotes; we shall avoid duplicating them here. Since the present volume is brief, mention should be made of more voluminous systematic treatments of the subject. William N. Loucks, *Comparative Economic Systems,* 7th ed. (New York: Harper & Row, 1965), is a veteran and venerable textbook, having held the field since 1938. It is particularly strong on institutional description. Carl Landauer, *Contemporary Economic Systems* (Philadelphia: Lippincott, 1964), also ranges broadly and is particularly strong on various aspects of socialism and planning. George N. Halm, *Economic Systems: A Comparative Analysis,* rev. ed. (New York: Holt, Rinehart, & Winston, 1960), emphasizes the contrast between market and command economies. Lynn Turgeon, *The Contrasting Economies: A Study of Modern Economic Systems* (Boston: Allyn & Bacon, paperback, 1963), is a sector-by-sector comparative analysis of the Soviet and American economies. The following are useful collections of readings: Morris Bornstein, *Comparative Economic Systems: Models and Cases* (Homewood, Ill.: Irwin, 1965); Marshall I. Goldman, *Comparative Economic Systems: A Reader* (New York: Random House, 1964); and Wayne A. Leeman, *Capitalism, Market Socialism, and Central Planning* (Boston: Houghton Mifflin, 1963). Most of these textbooks and collections of readings have substantial bibliographies.

Regarding "isms," we may add here references to one which was not discussed in the text for lack of space, African socialism. See William H. Friedland and Carl G. Rosberg, Jr. (eds.), *African Socialism* (Stanford: Stanford University Press, 1964); *Africa Report* (special issue on African socialism), Vol. 8, No. 5 (May, 1963); and Paul E. Sigmund, Jr. (ed.), *The Ideologies of the Developing Nations* (New York: Praeger, 1963).

Frederick Harbison and Charles A. Myers, *Management in the Industrial World: An International Analysis* (New York: McGraw-Hill, 1959), does just what the titles says, not omitting the USSR. More specifically, the following two books compare managers and management in the West and in the USSR: David Granick, *The Red Executive: A Study of the Organization Man in Russian Industry* (Garden City, N.Y.: Doubleday, 1960); and Richard N. Farmer and Barry M. Richman, *Comparative Management and Economic Progress* (Homewood, Ill.: Irwin, 1965). Jesse W. Markham has edited and contributed to a very useful collection on *The American Economy* (New York: Braziller, 1963), while Calvin B. Hoover is the editor of *Economic Systems of the Commonwealth* (Durham, N.C.: Duke Univ. Press, 1962). Also note Rudolf Frei (ed.), *Economic Systems of the West,* 2 volumes (Basel: List Gesellschaft, 1957, 1958).

P. Sargant Florence, *Industry and the State* (London: Hutchinson's University Library, 1957), is a concise introduction to the relations between the two in Britain and elsewhere. David McCord Wright, *Capitalism* (New York: McGraw-Hill, 1951; Gateway paperback, 1962), is a sympathetic analysis. Friedrich A. Hayek, *The Road to Serfdom* (Chicago: University of Chicago Press, 1944; also paperback), is a controversial classic defense of free-market capitalism. In a similar vein is Wilhelm Roepke, *Economics of the Free Society* (Chicago: Regnery, 1963). The symposium edited by Shigeto Tsuru, *Has Capitalism Changed?* (Tokyo: Iwanami Shoten, 1961), consists mostly of Marxist contributions of various shades plus J. K. Galbraith's reaffirmation of his theory of countervailing power. (See also the references scattered through Chapters 4 and 5.)

On the Soviet economy, in addition to the textbooks listed in Chapter 6, Note 1, see Nicolas Spulber, *The Soviet Economy* (New York: Norton, 1962); Franklyn D. Holzman (ed.), *Readings on the Soviet Economy* (Chicago: Rand McNally, 1962); and Morris Bornstein and Daniel R. Fusfeld (eds.), *The Soviet Economy: A Book of Readings* (Homewood, Ill.: Irwin, 1962). Soviet economic growth is carefully measured in Abram Bergson, *The Real National Income of Soviet Russia since 1928* (Cambridge: Harvard University Press, 1961), and Abram Bergson and Simon Kuznets (eds.), *Economic Trends in the Soviet Union* (Cambridge: Harvard University Press, 1963). Two recent studies of Soviet management, in addition to those cited above, are Barry M. Richman, *Soviet Management* (Englewood Cliffs, N.J.: Prentice-Hall, 1965); and Robert W. Campbell, *Accounting in Soviet Planning and Management* (Cambridge: Harvard University Press, 1963). An excellent study of an economy structurally very similar to the Soviet is John M. Montias, *Central Planning in Poland* (New Haven: Yale University Press, 1962).

Index